STRESS FOR SUCCESS

Also by David Lewis available from Carroll & Graf

The Secret Language of Success

STRESS FOR
SUCCESS

*Using Your Hidden Creative Energy for
Health, Achievement, and Happiness*

Dr. David Lewis

Carroll & Graf Publishers, Inc.
New York

First Carroll & Graf edition 1992

Carroll & Graf Publishers, Inc.
260 Fifth Avenue
New York, NY 10001

Library of Congress Cataloging-in-Publication Data is available.

ISBN: 0-88184-872-7

Manufactured in the United States of America

CONTENTS

ACKNOWLEDGMENTS

My grateful thanks to Cynthia Hemming for her valuable contributions in the production of this book, and to Patricia Jowsey MFPhys ITEC for assistance with those techniques dealing with aromatherapy and massage.

Should you read this book?
Take these two simple tests and then decide.

Test One: Clench your right hand.
Question: Did you hold your breath while doing so?

Test Two: Note the time. Now, without looking at your watch, estimate when sixty seconds has passed.
Question: Did you *underestimate* by 10 seconds or more?

If you answered YES to either of these questions, stress is causing you distress.

In this book I will explain how to make stress work for you, rather than against you. By mastering these quick and easy procedures for controlling stress, you can transform a potentially destructive force into a powerful ally, liberating hidden reserves of creative energy and enabling you to lead a happier, healthier, and more fulfilling life.

And all you need is just *60 seconds a day.*

INTRODUCTION
How to be Stressed
for Success

The techniques and exercises described will help you deal calmly and successfully with a wide range of situations which I have identified, through my work in business and industry, as highly stressful for a majority of people. Because all are easy to learn and can be used very rapidly, you'll be able to put them to work for you right away.

Continue working with a particular technique for a week to ten days, then review the situation.

Has it helped reduce or increase your stress to achieve the optimum level?

Has your confidence increased when tackling previously high-stress tasks?

Have anxiety symptoms, such as rapidly beating heart, dry mouth, and churning stomach decreased?

If you previously felt apathetic or quickly became fatigued by the task, are you now able to tackle it in a more alert and effective manner?

Hopefully you'll be able to answer "Yes" to these questions.

Continue using them, adding further techniques and exercises, as necessary, to combat excessive stress in other areas of your life. Continue working with the selected techniques until they become your immediate response to that type of stressful challenge.

1

How Stress Can Be Good for You

Centuries ago the word "stress" described the amount and type of physical torture needed to extract a confession. In medieval dungeons, inquisitors used thumbscrews to crush limbs by exerting compression stress. Victims were stretched on a rack, which produced tensile stress. The spikes of the Iron Maiden sliced through flesh, applying what engineers term shear stress.

Today, although excessive workloads, financial worries, family disputes, urban congestion, deadlines, and aggressive bosses have replaced the thumbscrew, rack, and Iron Maiden, most of us continue to regard stress as a form of torture, something so deadly dangerous and distressing that it has to be avoided at almost any cost.

Stress Gets a Bad Press

Stress is associated with virtually every human misery and misfortune. It's become one of the buzz words of modern life. You can't watch TV, listen to the radio, or read a newspaper without being warned that stress either causes or is caused by something bad. Stress has been blamed for virtually every complaint of modern life from premature ejaculation to absenteeism, from equipment downtime to early death.

There's no doubt about it. Stress gets a terrible press! This is not only unfair, but deeply misleading.

This bad press has led millions of men and women to flee from stress as though it were an invading army, to abandon careers they enjoyed and which brought them great satisfaction for the supposed tranquility of a rural lifestyle.

Yet the truth is we can never escape from stress, except at one very special time in our lives:

Death!

The Lifesaving Stress of Being Born

Birth is probably the most stressful experience we ever have to endure.

Consider our progress into this world. For several hours we are squeezed through the birth canal, sustaining severe pressure to the head, and being intermittently deprived of oxygen as the placenta and umbilical cord are compressed during uterine contractions. Suddenly we burst from the warm, life-sustaining protection of our mother's body into a harsh white, cold, odd-smelling environment of a hospital delivery room, where a giant holds us upside-down and slaps our buttocks!

No wonder that the brief journey from womb to world sends a baby's levels of the stress hormones adrenaline and noradrenaline soaring to a high not even found during a heart attack!

Yet without that stress we might not survive at all.

Far from being a terrible and dangerous ordeal, research shows that the stress of birth offers the best possible start in life.

Those hormones, belonging to a class of chemicals called

catecholamines, which enable us to fight or flee most effectively if we are faced by a perceived threat to survival, also prepare us for life outside the womb. They promote normal breathing by improving lung function, protect our heart and brain through increasing the blood flow to these vital organs, and stimulate production of the brain food glucose and the muscle food glycogen. By increasing the newborn's alertness, they even help ensure bonding between mother and child.

From the very first moments of independent life, therefore, stress proves essential and beneficial. If we learn how to control and use this potent force, it will remain powerful and will energize us throughout our lives.

Why Is Stress So Feared?

So how come the bad-guy image?

What makes the majority of us want to flee anything so potentially life-enhancing?

One problem lies in definitions.

Everybody thinks they know what stress is.

Few really do—and that includes a great many so-called specialists.

The word, which came into the English language during the fourteenth century, was originally used in the same way that engineers employ it today: to describe a force which produces strain.

Fowler's Modern English Usage defines stress as "mutual action exerted by contiguous bodies or parts and strain, or the alteration of form or dimensions produced by it."

That's right!

Until just after the Second World War, it was almost impossible to find a reference to stress as a psychological phenomenon in any of the academic literature. Since that time, the subject has expanded almost exponentially. A computer check of psychological abstracts between 1983 and 1991, published by the American Psychological Association, reveals more than 15,000 references under that heading. These range from a study of stress among "elite figure skaters" appearing in the *Journal of Sport and Exercise Psychology,* to research into stress and distress among classroom teachers published by the *Australian Journal of Educational Research.* Billions are now spent annually on stress research and stress prevention. Tens of thousands of new academic papers appear each year, adding to the miles of shelves devoted to the topic. The popular media can't leave it alone. And . . .

It All Started with Rats

Originally the "stress response" was defined specifically in terms of adrenal cortex enlargement, gastro-duodenal ulceration, and changes in the thymus gland found during postmortem examinations of laboratory rats.

Today doctors and scientists still talk about stress in terms of elevated hormone secretion—for example, cortisol from the adrenal cortex or adrenaline from the adrenal medulla; or increased autonomic nervous system activity, such as sweating, or changes in skin resistance, blood flow, pulse rate, or appetite, or diarrhea or amenorrhea.

Yet these physiological changes are clearly not what most people mean when they talk about being stressed. Many researchers, like Dr. Bruce Charlton, a lecturer in anatomy at the University of Glasgow, point to a troublesome circularity of definition.

A stressful stimulus is something which produces a stress response. But the stress response is also produced by a stressful stimulus! So the definition goes around and around, generating heat rather than light, and explaining nothing.

Another pitfall with this approach is it encourages us to look on stress as a single "thing" which can clearly be identified with a single cause, such as overwork or a bad marriage.

The danger of writing down even a lengthy list of causes is the assumption that if you get rid of these causes, you'll eliminate stress. This ignores the fact that virtually everything in the world can be identified as a source of stress at sometime or by someone. Furthermore, both a particular event and its exact opposite may cause stress. For example, having too little to do can be as stressful as trying to achieve too much. This duality is something I shall explore in more detail a little later.

Finally, many situations identified as very stressful can also produce considerable direct or indirect satisfaction. If you are given a poorly defined task to do, lack of direction may arouse anxiety and therefore prove highly stressful. Yet, having succeeded at the challenge, you will feel great pride and pleasure at a job well done through your own initiative.

Stress Is Good for You

The simple truth is this:

Stress, by which I mean anything which leads to changes in physical and mental arousal, can be either friend or foe. When used correctly, stress releases hidden reserves of creative energy, enabling you to enjoy a healthier, happier, and more successful life.

In this book I shall explain exactly how you can tap into those reserves through the use of easily mastered stress-control techniques, none of which will take more than a minute to perform.

2

The Power of
Positive Stress

Many years ago, Dr. Hans Selye, the father of modern stress research, distinguished between beneficial *eustress* (a word he coined from the Greek *eu* meaning "good," as in *euphoric)* and performance-sapping *distress.*

More recently, studies by Dr. Estelle Ramsey, a physiologist at Georgetown University Medical School, have shown that high achievers—men and women whose accomplishments have gained them a place in *Who's Who*—enjoy a longer and healthier life than the population as a whole. "These are among the most driven people in the world," Dr. Ramsey comments, "but, as a group, they're also among the healthiest."

History also shows us that many who have endured extremely stressful experiences are strengthened by their ordeal. Mahatma Gandhi, who led India to independence, spent more than 2,300 days behind bars and suffered several lengthy fasts, yet remained sufficiently healthy and vigorous to become one of the twentieth century's most influential leaders.

How is this possible?

To understand how we can be stressed for success, imagine a violin string. Too slack and you can't play a note. Too taut and the string is at risk of snapping.

Only under exactly the right amount of stress will the string yield beautiful music.

The same balance applies to stress. I call this optimum point our Peak Performance Stress Level (PPSL).

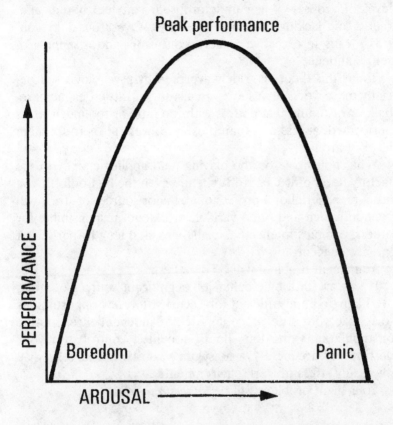

As you can see, up to a certain point increased arousal is associated with improved performance. But when we become aroused beyond this peak level, there is an often sudden and catastrophic decline in our ability and performance.

Peak Performance Stress

Several years ago, Russian sports psychologist Yuri Hanin suggested that athletic performance was linked to an optimal level of arousal. When underaroused, you feel bored, apathetic, and lacking in competitive spirit. Overarousal, by contrast, leads to excessive anxiety, confusion, and a sapping of self-confidence.

Today this theory is widely accepted by psychologists, especially those working in sports. In a study of Little League baseball, it was found that batters with too little or too much stress performed far less well than those who were at their optimum level of arousal.

What holds true on the playing field applies equally to the factory floor, office, boardroom, and even the bedroom! If you are a managerial or a professional, major sources of stress will include a high and often variable workload, responsibility for others, complex intellectual challenges, and lengthy periods of intense concentration.

Your main problem will be *overstress.*

If you are in a blue-collar job, significant sources of stress are likely to be insufficient job security, too few opportunities to realize your true potential, lack of independence, routine unstimulating work, long hours, too little control over your destiny and, frequently, a noisy, dirty, dusty, hot or otherwise physically stressful work environment.

Your main problem will be *understress.*

Your Peak Performance Stress Level (PPSL) Varies

When you are at PPSL, you feel energetic, enthusiastic, confident and, above all, in complete control of events. You react quickly and effectively. You become a creative and efficient problem solver. Recall of facts and figures is fast and accurate.

You feel alert and responsive. Your reaction time is fast, your control of fine muscles precise, your hand-eye coordination accurate. Your speed and endurance are optimum.

In short, you enjoy the type of sensation which psychologist Abraham Maslow identified as a "peak experience": one of those usually rare moments when everything seems to work perfectly, when you know for certain that your efforts will lead to success.

When your stress continues rising, however, your performance declines quickly. You become increasingly uncertain, anxious, confused, and unable to cope. Finally panic sets in.

PPSL Varies between Tasks

You require a *lower* stress level for intellectually demanding tasks, such as complex problem solving or decision making.

You need a *higher* level of stress when carrying out routine activities, such as production line work.

PPSL Varies among Individuals

A situation that one person finds intolerably stressful may leave another feeling only pleasantly stimulated. Many journalists need adrenaline-pumping deadlines in order to produce good copy. Some will even delay getting down to the task to increase the pressure.

How You Can Be Stressed for Success

First identify your Peak Performance Stress Level for a particular task.

Second, maintain that Peak Level throughout the task.

The rest of this book will show you how to do just that using techniques which take no more than sixty seconds to perform.

3

A Sixty-second What?

When I tell my clients that they can control their stress—and use it creatively—in around a minute a day, their first response is usually disbelief. Their second is irritation. They think I'm taking their stress difficulties a great deal too lightly.

"I have a terrible boss, a shaky marriage, my teenage kids don't understand me, my commute to work each day leaves me exhausted, my love life is nonexistent, my debts are enormous and even my dog doesn't love me. And you have the nerve to tell me all my problems can be solved in sixty seconds a day. How dare you!"

By way of reply, I often drop a lighted match onto some cotton placed in a large metal ashtray on my office desk. Because it's been soaked in alcohol, the cotton flares up, then burns steadily.

Taking a glass from my desk, I pour a small amount of water over the flames, which are quenched immediately.

"A small fire can be brought under control quickly and easily," I point out. "But suppose those flames had been allowed to spread unchecked. In no time papers on the desk would start burning, then the desk, then the room. In a short while, the whole building might have burned up. Then it would have taken hours to put out the flames. We'd have had to send for firefighters. Tremendous damage would have been caused. The building might have been damaged beyond repair."

I go on to explain that fire and stress have much in common. Both are potentially destructive forces capable of human control. Uncontrolled, fire sweeps through forests or rampages through buildings, leaving death and devastation in its wake. Controlled, fire provides the energy to drive industry, heat our homes, power our cars, fly our jets, and cook our food.

Similarly, controlled stress is a potent source of creative energy which allows us to work with maximum efficiency.

Neither fire nor stress is easy to bring under control when allowed to burn unchecked for too long.

The moral is simple.

Allow stress to get out of hand, and you'll eventually burn out. Catch and control stress early enough, and you will transform it into a creative power. As the Chinese sage Lao-Tse wisely remarked: "The biggest problem in the world could have been solved easily when it was small."

4

Why Stress Cures Can
Increase Your Stress

Before getting down to the meat of this book, let me address one issue which is often raised by my clients:

Are all the methods around for controlling stress equally effective?

You see, many of my clients are victims of failed treatments. They have tried in the past to control stress using a wide variety of techniques from relaxation to hypnotherapy, and Autogenic Training (the repetition of relaxing phrases) to meditation.

Don't get me wrong. Most of these are great techniques. For some people, they provide the perfect answer to controlling stress.

For others, they are anything but an antidote to stress. In fact, they can end up leaving some people feeling even more stressed and unhappy than before.

To see how and why this happens, let me describe the experiences of two of my clients.

George, a World-class Type A

When we first met, George, age 45, regularly worked an 80-hour week in his job as vice-president of a software company. During a typical seven-day work week, he'd be juggling tight production schedules, worrying about cash flow, and fighting for orders in an increasingly cutthroat market. On top of all this, George traveled constantly, visiting clients and suppliers in Europe and Japan.

Aggressive, competitive, and ambitious George was exactly the kind of individual that cardiologist Meyer Friedman, director of the Recurrent Coronary Prevention Project in San Francisco, has identified as a Type A. Only George was even more so. In fact, George was a world-class Type A, for life just wasn't fast enough. George had turned impatience into an art form. He hated any kind of delay. In restaurants, waiters served him on the double or risked a furious tirade. Even if he really wanted something, he'd storm out of a busy store rather than wait to be served. Once, riding with him in a New York express elevator, I watched as George tapped irritably at his watch. It was clear that even those few seconds of enforced idleness were unbearable to him!

Yet, despite the pressure, George loved his fast-track lifestyle and refused to accept that it could ever harm him. "I don't suffer from stress," he once boasted to me. "I'm a carrier!"

But George was wrong—so wrong it almost killed him.

George had been misled by the widely held belief that if you really enjoy what you do, work stress can't ever get to you, that somehow your love for your job offers absolute protection.

Unfortunately, this is like saying that if you adore eating and drinking, gluttony will never harm your health. A month before George consulted me, a routine medical check revealed him to be severely hypertensive, with blood pressure of 156/100.

That's way too high, and George was rightly worried. Such

hypertension significantly increased the risk of heart disease and kidney failure, while reducing his life expectancy by up to twelve years.

So when his doctor suggested that he try Progressive Relaxation, George agreed immediately. Progressive Relaxation, which involves first tensing and then relaxing each of your major muscle groups in turn, was developed some fifty years ago by University of Chicago physiologist Edmund Jacobson. Studies have shown this widely used procedure lowers blood pressure, reduces tension, and creates a more tranquil state of mind. Progressive Relaxation takes about three weeks to learn and requires regular sessions, each lasting around 30 minutes, to bring about worthwhile results.

For some people, Progressive Relaxation is extremely beneficial. Unfortunately, George was not one of them. In fact, it ended up making him even more stressed than before.

"My doctor gave me a tape cassette of instructions," he recalls. "I started working with it the moment I returned home. But after only a few minutes I found myself getting more and more tense and anxious. My mind started racing so fast that it was impossible to concentrate on the tape. The more I tried to unwind, the more uptight I felt. I called my doctor, and she said to keep on going, that it was natural to get more tense at first. But I couldn't just lie there. It was sheer torture. After ten days, finding my blood pressure had actually risen a couple of points, I tossed out the cassette and abandoned all hope of controlling stress through relaxation."

Shortly afterward George consulted me and learned some of the one-minute stress-control procedures described in this book.

Today, without any major lifestyle changes, George's blood pressure is a healthier 130/85. He no longer suffers from poor digestion or low back pain, and he enjoys more restful sleep. At work, both his problem-solving and decision-making abilities have improved significantly.

Equally important is George's ability to deal calmly with

challenges which once sent his stress soaring way above peak performance levels.

George's problem is far from rare. The more impatient and competitive people are, the more difficulty they will have in mastering Progressive Relaxation—or, indeed, any technique involving lengthy training and regular practice.

A similar difficulty confronted another of my clients when she suffered a stress-induced psychological problem.

Susan, a Two-shift Career Woman

Like many ambitious career women Susan, a 33-year-old advertising executive and mother of two daughters, worked two shifts: the first at work, the second when she returned home in the evening. From dawn's early light to lights out, her every activity had to be tightly scheduled. "I used to joke that the only way I could get sick was if it had been timetabled in my appointment book," she recalls.

Like George, for years Susan appeared to thrive on her demanding lifestyle. "I kept fit, got up around five o'clock every day, winter and summer, to go swimming. I played squash three times a week and took aerobics classes regularly," she told me. "I was so healthy that it never occurred to me I could fall victim to stress."

Susan had been misled by a second widely held myth about stress: that being fit prevents your ever getting stressed. In fact, your fitness may even make matters worse.

Because you appear so much better able to cope with a high workload than the less fit people around you, there's a strong temptation on the part of bosses to dump all the most stressful challenges into your in-basket.

"I was always given the toughest assignments," says Susan, "because my boss believed I coped with them better than anyone else in the company. If there was an angry client to pacify, it was me they sent for. If there was a rush job to complete, I was always first in line to be asked. I became the agency's troubleshooter, always in the middle of a firefight."

Because Susan was in such excellent physical health, she was able to work long and hard for years. Then, without warning, everything changed.

"I woke up one Monday morning and immediately suffered a panic attack. I'd never experienced anything like it before and felt terrified. My heart was thumping so fast I felt certain I was having a major heart attack. My husband called our doctor, who could find nothing wrong. An electrocardiogram confirmed that my heart was in great shape. The only problem was, I wasn't.

"From that morning on, for more than a year, each day was a nightmare. At work I found it hard to make the simplest decisions. My creativity simply nosedived. I wasn't able to cope with tasks which, only a couple of weeks before, I'd have tackled with ease. My confidence was shot to pieces. Just getting up in the morning was a major effort."

At her doctor's suggestion Susan agreed to attend classes in Autogenics.

Developed during the 1930s by Dr. J. W. Schultz, a German neuropsychologist, Autogenic Training (AT) teaches learning to relax by repeating such phrases as "My hands and arms are heavy and warm. . . . My breathing is deep and even. . . ." As with Progressive Relaxation, Autogenic Training can be a powerful stress-management technique.

But with Susan, as with George, AT proved anything but helpful. "My problem was finding the time to attend regular classes. It was a thirty-minute drive to the AT training center, and each session lasted around one hour. The only way I could fit this in was by giving up my squash and cutting down on swimming. Without this regular exercise, I became increasingly tense. After I'd missed a couple of sessions because my daughter had fallen ill, I decided to give up."

Neither Progressive Relaxation nor Autogenic Training are ineffectual procedures. They can, in fact, be very useful. But for many people who most need to control their stress, they are simply impractical because they take too long. This may be one reason why although 72 percent of men and 40 percent of women report feeling chronically stressed, only a tiny minority ever make any serious attempts to control that stress.

Is Your Stress Response Like George's and Susan's?

It's not that these widely used therapeutic procedures are ineffectual.

Far from it. For many, they provide an excellent answer to managing stress.

But, in my professional experience, there are also a substantial number of sufferers who are not helped at all by them. In fact, they are made even more stressed by these lengthy, time-consuming treatments. Then, to make matters worse, they despair of ever being able to bring performance-zapping, health-destroying, relationship-wrecking, stress under control.

If, in my test at the beginning of this book, you underestimated the passing of one minute by 10 seconds or more, if you loathe waiting in line, rapidly become irritated by even trivial delays, and fume when trapped in traffic, it's likely that your response will be the same as those of George and Susan.

Maybe you have even tried Progressive Relaxation, AT, or some other form of stress-management procedure without success.

If so, don't worry.

The techniques I teach have worked for hundreds of sufferers.

They will be equally helpful to you.

They are all easy to learn and quick to use.

You can carry them out during what would be otherwise be wasted moments.

· When commuting to work.
· Waiting at a stop light while driving.
· In the few moments before rising to deliver a speech.
· Prior to a difficult meeting.
· During your midmorning or afternoon breaks.
· When you are delayed at an airport or during the flight itself.

Performed immediately before or even during a stressful situation, they will make it far easier to stay cool, calm, and confident. You can also use them to unwind following a stressful encounter to prevent your carrying performance-harming tension into your next activity.

By spending 60 seconds destressing yourself at the end of a hectic day, you can avoid taking work-related stresses home with you.

Controlling stress this way does more than safeguard your health. It also increases your chances of success by ensuring that you will perform every task with exactly the right level of mental and physical alertness.

5

The Nature of Stress

Negative stress occurs whenever the demands being made on you are greater than your ability to cope.

There are three ways this can happen.

Stresses Affecting Many People

Some stressors affect hundreds or even thousands of people at the same time, such as natural and man-made disasters: earthquakes, hurricanes, wars, riots, and train or airplane crashes.

Stresses Affecting Smaller Groups

A second type of stress is shared by smaller groups, people who are related to one another in some way, like factory workers threatened by layoffs or a family suffering bereavement. Major life events, such as relocation, the end of an intimate relationship, serious illness of a loved one, children leaving home, being fired, retirement and, especially, bereavement create significant increases in this type of stress.

Stresses Affecting Individuals

Finally, there are the very personal stresses we endure as individuals, the majority of which are due to the hassles of life, such as commuting, aggressive clients, conflicts between career and family, working in noisy surroundings, and so on.

During the 1960s two American psychologists, Thomas Holmes and Richard Rahe, constructed a list of the most stressful events we can experience. These were then rated by the amount of stress they imposed.

EVENT	RATING
Death of spouse	100
Divorce	73
Marital separation	65
Personal injury	53
Marriage	50
Being fired	47
Retirement	45
Sexual difficulties	39
High mortgage	31
Child leaving home	29

As you can see, although the loss of a loved one heads the list by a high margin, even events normally thought of as joyful, such as marriage, are also stressful.

The Nature of Workplace Stress

Research has shown that the most stressful organizations are those which combine highly competitive cultures with demands for total dedication. Today that means the vast majority of successful companies.

Asked to list the qualities needed for corporate success, 93 percent of bosses made "total commitment" their top qualification, while 75 percent said a highly competitive nature was essential for climbing the corporate ladder.

But it's not only high-flying executive employment which creates excessive stress. According to a recent U.S. study, ten of the most stressful jobs are:

Inner-city teacher
Police officer
Miner
Air-traffic controller
Medical intern
Stockbroker
Journalist
Customer service/complaint-department worker
Waitress
Secretary

The same survey revealed that 64 percent of employers regard excessive stress as the number-one health threat facing their company.

They are right. A study by Northwestern National Life Insurance of 600 workers showed that 46 percent felt their jobs were highly stressful, and 34 percent felt so stressed that they were seriously thinking of quitting.

Research indicates that around half of all absence from work can be blamed on stress-related illness. It has been estimated to affect 1.4 percent of the workforce at any one time and to cause at least 13 percent of all sickness.

More than 40 million working days are lost annually through stress-related health problems, and the figure is rising. Stress-related compensation claims account for 14 percent of occupational disease, up from less than 5 percent in 1980.

Stress and Disease

When we become stressed, our adrenal glands, located above the kidneys, release adrenaline and noradrenaline into our bloodstream. These powerfully stimulating hormones, which are also produced by nerve cells, act as chemical messengers. Nerves releasing noradrenaline affect almost every organ in the body, including the eye, stomach, intestines, bladder, tonsils, and appendix.

People who have abnormally high levels of noradrenaline, caused by malfunctioning adrenal glands, have an above-average risk of coronary disease. Some doctors believe that chronic stress has a similarly damaging effect on the heart.

Dr. Robert Karasek, of the University of Southern California, matched incidence of past heart attacks in more than 4,800 men with the work they did. While the incidence of heart attacks in the entire sample was only 1.5 percent, the rate among men with high-stress jobs was almost three times as high.

In a study of resistance to illness, Dr. Kiecolt-Glaser reported a decrease in the number of lymphocytes (white blood cells that are key players in the immune system) among medical students on the first day of their final exams. She also found that, during their exams, the students had diminished immune-response activity as well as a drastically reduced ability to produce the vital defense chemical interferon.

Dr. Joseph Schwartz, a sociologist at the State University of New York at Stony Brook, believes that the key factor in determining the amount of work-related stress is control. "How much freedom a worker has in deciding how to meet a boss's demands will determine if those demands actually produce stress."

It is this independence—this freedom to regulate the significant events in one's life—which I believe lies at the very core of effective stress control.

Stress and Control

After an earthquake or other major disaster, survivors are often so shocked that they remain apathetically beside their shattered homes, without even bothering to find food or seek shelter. Rescue workers, such as doctors, nurses and firefighters, who also live in the disaster zone, are able to function efficiently under the same traumatic circumstances because rigorous training enables them to retain a sense of exerting control over events.

By contrast, the victims can do little to influence events. And in this inability lies the major cause of their debilitating stress.

Stress comes in many guises, as these brief extracts from recent client files demonstrate:

". . . I have grown used to dealing with frantic deadlines, but this doesn't mean the stress gets any better. At the end of most weeks I feel absolutely drained."

Advertising Copy Writer—Age 29

"There is never enough time in the day to get done all that's expected of me. When I get home I'm exhausted, yet find it almost impossible to sleep. My health is suffering. I feel constantly tired out."

Financial Consultant—Age 52

"I've seen a number of my colleagues burn out by the age of thirty, and time pressures are a big factor. It some-

times seems I'm running at top speed just to stay one step
ahead of the game."

Sales Representative—Age 26

"I enjoy a fast-paced life. But there are still moments of
blind panic when I think of all that has to be done in the
time available."

Television Producer—Age 37

"I would say that making time, finding time, stretching
time to fit in all the demands made on me is my number-
one source of stress."

CEO of Manufacturing Company—Age 42

Behind these very different descriptions of stress lies a single factor: the fear of losing control. That feeling of inadequacy which arises when nothing we do makes much difference to what happens.

When all our efforts come to nothing.

When every expectation is confounded.

When every hope is dashed.

Whether or not you become overly stressed in any given
situation, therefore, depends almost entirely on the degree of
control you can realistically exert over events.

Stress isn't out there, stress arises from within! It stems from
the interaction between what happens and your perception of
what is happening.

Drop a scorpion into a box of puppies, and you get highly
stressed dogs. Drop a scorpion into a box of elf owls, which
look on them as a delicacy, and what you get is lunch!

6

Balancing Your
Stress Budget

Using stress creatively can be compared to handling your finances prudently.

Let's return to the description of stress with which I started the last chapter. Negative stress occurs whenever the demands being made on you are greater than your ability to cope.

Exactly the same could be said about managing your finances. Spend more than you've got and, sooner or later—usually sooner—your extravagance will catch up with you. As Charles Dickens's Mr. Micawber put it: "Annual income twenty pounds, annual expenditure nineteen nineteen six, result happiness. Annual income twenty pounds, annual expenditure twenty pounds ought and six, result misery."

Get Stressed—Pay the Price

To pay for stress, we draw on reserves of what I call our Stress Resistance Currency (SRC). Each time you get stressed, you pay out a sum in this currency. Unless you replenish your reserves, you will get into stress debt. And that's when problems start.

Let's imagine that you start your working week with 100 units of Stress Resistance Currency.

These have been built up during a relaxing weekend.

Here's how you spend reserves:

Activity	Cost	Balance
Breakfast argument with your spouse	5	95
Driving to work through heavy traffic	10	85
Dealing with the normal hassles of work	20	65
Afternoon crisis in the office	35	30
Driving home	10	20

You return home with some currency still in reserve.

Now picture a very different scenario.

Activity	Cost	Balance
Breakfast argument with spouse and son	10	90
Argument with other driver	25	65
Disagreement with secretary	10	55
Daily hassles	20	35
Major crisis	35	00
Fight on returning home	15	−15

You have overspent your reserves by 15 units.

On Tuesday, after a restless night, you are overdrawn before getting out of bed. At this point real trouble can start.

In most of these situations, spending your SRCs did nothing to improve your situation and in many cases probably made matters worse. You squandered finite reserves for no good reason. This doesn't mean that you should never stand up for yourself, argue, express an honest opinion, or lose your temper. If that's what you feel like doing go ahead.

But always bear in mind that there will be a price that must be paid.

The first rule of sixty-second stress control is simple. Consider each potentially stressful situation as a business transaction. Before drawing on your limited reserves, ask yourself if the return on investment is likely to be worthwhile.

Imagine that your Stress Resistance Currency is real money, hard-earned savings.

Say to yourself: "This is going to cost me X units of stress currency." Place an arbitrary figure on the experience, depending on how stressful it's likely to prove.

Now ask yourself, just as you would before any important purchase: "Is it worth the price? Am I getting a fair return on my investment?" Is the expenditure going to yield a practical benefit you cannot obtain in any other way?

Reflect on possible alternatives.

Can you negotiate a better deal?

Could you achieve a similar result in a more cost-effective way?

Are you frustrated by slow traffic? You could rage at other motorists. Or you might decide to take a break and use one of the fast winding-down techniques described in the following chapters before continuing with your journey. You might put on a tape of relaxing music, or distract yourself with a comedy program on the radio.

Spend or save? Squander or conserve?

The choice is always yours.

But bear in mind the old Spanish proverb: "Take what you want from life, says God. And pay the price!"

By now the basic philosophy behind being stressed for success should be clear.

First, controlled stress is highly beneficial because it allows us to function, mentally and physically, at our peak of performance.

Next, in maintaining this peak level, we spend our reserves of Stress Resistance Currency (SRC).

To sustain an optimum level of stress, we must always maintain a reserve of SRC. We can do this in two ways: by not squandering our reserves needlessly, in situations where becoming angry or upset will not do the slightest good; and by both replenishing diminished reserves and increasing these reserves by using the techniques which I shall describe in later chapters.

In order to do any of these we must first be able to monitor our levels of stress with a fair degree of accuracy.

7

Monitoring Your Stress

A rule of thumb for deciding whether your stress has risen above or fallen below your Peak Performance Level is to ask yourself: "When tackling this task or dealing with this situation, do I feel confident and capable, excessively anxious, or largely apathetic, over the outcome?"

If you welcome the challenge, enjoy what you are doing, and perform to the best of your ability, your stress level is close to your Peak Performance Level.

When your performance fails because of anxiety or an inability to concentrate, chances are that the stress generated is too high. If you couldn't care less about the task and are motivated mainly by the need for reward or fear or failure, your stress levels are probably too low.

This subjective approach is used widely, although the reasons why stress is occurring are seldom fully appreciated. Knowing what to do about stress is even less frequently understood.

Unfortunately, this approach has some problems. On a number of occasions, you may fail to notice significant increases in stress. You may not realize the increase in one of four common situations:

1. When Stress Builds Gradually

Imagine a half-filled glass of water. There is ample space to pour in additional fluid without any risk of overflow.

Now picture the glass placed under a dripping faucet. The level rises slowly but surely until the water is lapping at the rim. Once this point has been reached, it needs only one more drop for the glass to overflow.

The same can happen with gradually building stress. If levels rise gradually, you may find yourself tipped over your Peak Performance Level by even a fairly minor additional stress.

This is what happened to Martin, an experienced and well-regarded lawyer. Normally easygoing and relaxed, 26-year-old Martin had suffered a series of relatively minor stresses over the course of two weeks. His wife, away nursing her widowed mother, had left him to look after their four-year-old twin boys. The morning Martin's stress glass finally overflowed their maid arrived late, his car refused to start, there was a large and unexpected bill in the mail, he had cut himself shaving, and his wife phoned to say she wouldn't be home that weekend, as expected, because her mother was not well enough to be left alone.

Martin's normally well-ordered life was coming unraveled. His control was slipping. He reached his office with little capacity to absorb further stress and discovered that an appointment blunder had left him with thirty minutes to cross town for an important conference with a major client. Having reached his client's offices with only seconds to spare, Martin then discovered that important papers had been omitted from the file.

A calm and collected Martin would have simply phoned his secretary and told her to fax them over. But this incident was the final drop which caused his glass to overflow.

Martin's stress level rose abruptly. Angry and confused, he stopped thinking straight, tried bluffing his way through the conference, and failed miserably. As a result, he almost lost a top client, and he left the meeting embarrassed and demoralized.

Had Martin known about the Rapid Stress Control procedures he was later to learn, that buildup of stress could have been avoided. He would have known how to keep the water in his glass at a level where there was little risk of overflow.

2. *When Stress Builds Suddenly*

If something goes unexpectedly wrong while you are performing a task that you normally handle well within your PPSL, an abrupt and catastrophic rise in stress may occur.

The illusion below, called the Necker Cube, illustrates the speed with which this transition from Peak Performance Level to a hyperstressed state can occur.

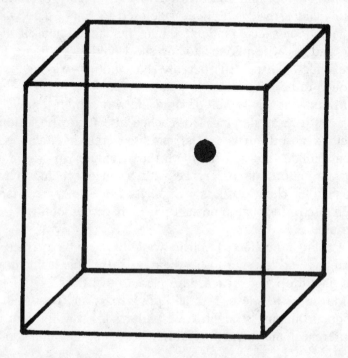

Look steadily at the drawing. The dot suddenly changes its position. The switch is what mathematicians call "discontinuous." There is no halfway point at which you can stop the dot's motion. You cannot even catch the dot moving. One moment it is in the middle of the cube's upper surface, the next toward the top right of the front face.

Sudden changes in stress levels can be as discontinuous. One moment you are confident and in control. The next, panic has set in. This happened to a colleague of mine, a well-known British psychologist who was presenting a paper on—ironically enough—stress management, at an international conference. Everything was fine until he rose to face the audience. "Up to that point I had felt slightly apprehensive, but no more anxious than normal when making a presentation. Then, suddenly, as I stared out across the auditorium, I panicked."

Fortunately he had the skill—and sufficient composure—to admit as much to his surprised audience. "I told them I was having a panic attack, which I would have to bring under control before continuing," he says. "I then turned my back on them, went through a rapid stress-control technique, overcame the problem, and completed my presentation without further difficulty."

Although many of his listeners were convinced that his panic attack was a stunt, my colleague assured me that his sudden surge in stress levels was both genuine and as unexpected as it had been unwelcome.

3. Stress Can Be Hidden

A third difficulty arises with activities which, although creating high stress, are not seen by you as especially stressful. This applies particularly to tasks you greatly enjoy. Here, as with my client George, the pleasure the activity provides conceals the degree of stress involved.

4. Stress Can Be Ignored

For many years, the Third Avenue elevated trains ran through New York City. Then the line was closed down and the rails torn up. Not long after, police began receiving early-morning phone calls from people living alongside the now-abandoned track. They were complaining of strange sounds in the night, odd and inexplicable noises that woke them from sleep.

It was no coincidence that most of these calls were received around the time the first trains in the morning would have started running. Residents were being disturbed *not by noise, but by silence.* After years of living beside the track they had learned to ignore the noise of passing trains. But silence was new and strange.

Live with chronic stress long enough and, like passing trains, you stop noticing—until the day dawns when your mind or body serve notice that something has gone badly wrong.

Sometimes the malfunction is physical, like my client George's hypertension. On other occasions, the reaction is primarily emotional, as with Susan's early-morning panics.

One of the most destructive results of chronic stress is Burn Out Stress Syndrome or BOSS, a "psychological withdrawal from work in response to excessive stress." BOSS's many ill-effects include

- Extreme reluctance to go to work each day
- Profound sense of failure
- Anger and resentment
- Guilt, cynicism, and self-blame
- Intense fatigue, even on waking
- Sleep and eating disorders
- Depression, low morale, feeling of hopelessness
- Loss of confidence and low self-esteem
- Increased consumption of cigarettes, alcohol, and drugs, both medically prescribed and otherwise

· Increased frequency of colds and flu, headaches, gas-
  trointestinal disorders, back pains, and missed men-
  strual periods.

Once established, BOSS becomes a self-reinforcing process,
as the negative attitudes and actions which result lead to further depression.

To prevent BOSS, monitor your stress levels on a regular
basis using the techniques described in the following chapters.

8

Monitoring Workplace Stress

This quiz enables you to compare your current levels of stress with the average for your occupation. Repeat it every few months, or any time there are significant changes in your working situation.

How to Take This Quiz

Answer the following 15 questions by choosing one of the responses and scoring accordingly.

Response	Score
Does Not Apply	0
Never	1
Rarely	2
Sometimes	3
Often	4
Nearly All the Time	5

How Frequently Do You . . .

1. Find yourself without the authority to carry out all the responsibilities placed on you?

2. Have difficulty getting hold of the facts and figures needed to do your job efficiently?

3. Feel uncertain about the scope and responsibilities of your job?

4. Have such a heavy workload that it is impossible to complete all the tasks demanded of you during a normal working day?

5. Find yourself unable to satisfy the conflicting demands of various people in your life?

6. Not really know what your supervisor or immediate superior thinks about you or how your performance is being evaluated?

7. Worry about the decisions you make which affect the lives of those working with you?

8. Fail to influence your superior's decisions or actions even though these affect you?

9. Find the demands of your job interfering with your personal or family life?

10. Believe that your job requires you to do things which are against your better judgment?

11. Feel uncertain what is expected of you by your colleagues or superiors?

12. Find that the volume of your work makes it impossible to do those tasks as well as you like?

13. Consider yourself insufficiently qualified to cope with the demands of your job?

14. Feel that you are not well liked or accepted by those with whom you work?

15. Find yourself unclear about which opportunities for promotion or advancement exist within your job?

How to Score This Quiz

Start by adding up your score. Next, note how many question were answered "Does Not Apply." As these are clearly irrelevant to you, you can ignore them and remove them from your final calculation. *Subtract* the number of questions you gave a zero score from the total number of questions asked (15).

Suppose you gave 6 questions a zero score because they do not apply. Then you have 9 relevant questions.

Now divide your total score by the number of relevant questions and compare this with the average score for your particular occupation on the chart below.

Two examples will help make the method clear.

Example #1

Suppose your total score is 59. Three of the 15 questions received a 0 score because they did not apply. This leaves 12 relevant questions. Your stress score is calculated by dividing 59 by 12, or 4.9.

This reveals a stress level well above average for all occupations.

Example #2

Your score is 18 and you replied "Does Not Apply" to 2 out of 15 questions, so 13 were relevant. Dividing 18 by 13 gives 1.4, a stress score below those for all occupations.

Stress Chart

Occupation	Stress Levels		
	Normal	Moderate	High
Professional, technical	2.0	2.5+	3.5+
Managerial	1.8	2.3+	3.3+
Clerical, sales	1.8	2.3+	3.3+

Occupation	Stress Levels		
	Normal	Moderate	High
Craftsmen, foremen	1.7	2.2+	3.2+
Semiskilled/unskilled	1.5	2.0+	3.0+

If your stress score was on the high side, don't worry. The techniques described in this book will help you reduce your overall stress level fairly rapidly.

If your score was average or even slightly below average for your occupation, chronic stress is not presently causing you any problems. However, it's a good idea to repeat this test every few months to check that changing circumstances have not increased your overall stress.

Where no chronic stress exists, it is still perfectly possible to suffer high levels of acute stress in certain situations.

9

Stress and Your Personality

As I have already explained, a situation which one person may find intolerably stressful will seem agreeably challenging to another. To understand the way work-related stress especially affects you, we must explore the interplay between your personality and your job. Unless your job changes significantly, this assessment need be carried out only once.

Assessing Your Personality Type

Choose one of the four symbols on the following page which seems to best represent your personality. Make your choice rapidly, without analyzing the designs; your instant response is most revealing.

What Your Choice Reveals

Triangle: You are happiest organizing and directing others. This symbol is first choice of movers and shakers. Your strength lies in setting and achieving clearly defined goals. *Triangles* can often be identified by their use of such phrases as "Our objective is," "We must strike while the iron is hot," and "right on target."

Circle: You are at your best dealing with people. Your intuition and empathy help you win cooperation from others. Your strength lies in resolving conflicts and creating a friendly working atmosphere. *Circles* tend to make such comments as "I feel that," "My intuition suggests," and "I have a hunch that . . ."

Square: You adopt an intellectual approach to life's challenges. Objective and logical, you favor reasoned arguments, and you base your decisions on a careful appraisal of the situation. Your strength lies in being able to make sense of complex information. *Squares* use remarks like "The facts are," "Logic compels us to conclude that," and "Reason dictates that we . . ."

Squiggle: This choice suggests an abundance of energy and enthusiasm. You thrive on novelty and unfamiliar challenges. Your strength is the ability to motivate others by generating excitement for new projects. *Squiggles* favor phrases suggesting energy and excitement, like "Making great strides," "soaring ahead," and "fantastic potential."

About This Assessment

Although quick and easy to complete, this projective test based on personality types, developed by the Swiss psychiatrist Carl Jung, has proved remarkably accurate.

Now, to assess your workplace stress, examine how your personality profile responds to different types of occupation. The wide range of potential careers may be placed in one of three categories:

Commanders include all those who initiate, organize, supervise, control, or direct the activities of others. They include CEOs and executives, managers, officials, supervisors, and foremen.

Creators are concerned with turning ideas into reality: everyone who makes something, from a blueprint to an automobile, a new drug to a skyscraper. This group includes artists, craftsmen, engineers, builders, designers, production-line workers, scientists, and technicians.

Communicators are in the business of telling and/or selling. They usually seek to convey not merely the facts about a product or service, but interest, excitement, and involvement. This category includes teachers, actors and actresses, authors, film directors, advertising copywriters, public-relations consultants, therapists, doctors, nurses, and psychologists.

Frequently an occupation can be placed in more than one of the above categories. If this applies to your work, decide which activity—Commanding, Creating, or Communicating—takes up the greatest part of your working day and read the comments under that heading.

If you divide your time more or less equally among several occupations, this analysis will still help you discover whether one of these is generating more stress than the others, and a possible explanation of why this may be so.

One of my clients, who was both a teacher and a department head, found that his work in class aroused only positive feelings. While teaching, he felt fulfilled and agreeably stimulated by the challenge. He was working at his Peak Performance Stress Level (PPSL).

But his dislike of giving orders and organizing others led to negative stress all the time he wore his supervisor's hat. During the time he carried out these tasks, his stress rose well above his PPSL.

In addition to describing the different types of stress, I have included some brief suggestions for reducing or increasing stress levels to bring them closer to your PPSL. These notes should be used together with the detailed explanation of stress-control procedures described in later chapters.

Work Category Commanders *Personality Symbol* Triangle

Stress is likely to increases sharply if anything comes between you and an important career goal—for example, if an equally determined colleague attempts to achieve his or her ambitions at your expense, or if subordinates make mistakes.

Managing Your Stress

Without attempting to be any less ambitious, try to adopt a more relaxed approach to life. Instead of flying off the handle or getting depressed when confronted by obstacles to your progress, try to remain calm and collected. Avoid narrowing your range of interests by going after only work goals. Enjoying a full and satisfying social and family life is just as important as career success.

Work Category Commanders Personality Symbol Circle

Sensitivity to other people's feelings and the ability intuitively to put yourself in their shoes means that making tough decisions, which adversely affect the lives of others, will prove highly stressful. Aggressive encounters with subordinates, disputes with colleagues, or any other interpersonal conflict will cause your stress levels to rise sharply. Difficulties may also occur at home as you try to satisfy both your need for a close family life and the demands of your work.

Managing Your Stress

Whenever possible, reduce your stress by delegating those tasks that you find especially stressful. In addition, try to develop the ability to remain emotionally detached when carrying through a necessary plan of action.

Work Category Commanders Personality Symbol Square

A major cause of your negative stress is likely to be your trust in the power of reason to resolve conflicts. When others fail to be persuaded by what seems logical evidence, you may find yourself becoming frustrated and angry. Don't assume that because *you* can clearly see all the benefits of such an objective approach, others will automatically share your vision.

Managing Your Stress

If you tend to bottle up your feelings, begin showing your emotions more openly. If you are justifiably angry or upset, allow yourself to express these feelings.

Bear in mind that *Circles* are swayed more by emotions than logic, *Squiggles* want to feel excited and enthused by a project, rather than submerged beneath a mountain of facts and figures, and that *Triangles* are impressed by a clear sense of purpose and direction.

Work Category Commanders *Personality Symbol* Squiggle

When others fail to share your excitement for a proposed new development or fail to become sufficiently enthusiastic about one of your pet schemes, your stress levels can rise sharply. You may find yourself getting angry at their apparent inability to share your vision, or frustrated by their caution. When you are in a position of power, your instinct may be to compel obedience in the hope that once a project has got underway, your subordinates will start to become equally involved. This strategy seldom works, and the most likely consequence is barely concealed frustration and even a desire to sabotage your efforts.

Managing Your Stress

Pace yourself so that you don't run out of energy and simply abandon your plans. At home don't allow yourself to become overly upset if other members of the family aren't always as enthused by novel ideas as you are.

Organize your life so that there are always plenty of new things happening, with many novel projects and schemes at various stages of development. This helps to cushion you against inevitable setbacks and disappointments. Remember that *Squares* are best appealed to through logical arguments based on a careful, objective analysis of the situation, *Circles* need an appeal to their emotions as much as their intellect, while *Triangles* will want to see a clear plan of action for implementing key goals.

Work Category Creators *Personality Symbol* Triangle

A major source of your stress is the inability to exercise sufficient control over projects and the frustration of getting blamed for mistakes outside your control. You see how tasks could be performed more efficiently, yet are unable to persuade superiors to accept these views. Conflicts are most likely with other *Triangles,* who will have their own very firm ideas about how things should be done.

Managing Your Stress

Try to achieve as much freedom as possible, so that you are able to take your own decisions—for example, by gaining greater authority and responsibility. Since you will often find your drive to control events thwarted, it is also important for you to adopt a relaxed approach to life and not to allow frustrations to build.

If you are powerless to make desired changes at work and there seems little prospect of things changing in the near future, take up a sport or hobby where *you* can set tough but achievable goals.

Work Category Creators
Personality Symbol Squares

Your stress rises when others reach poorly reasoned conclusions or make illogical decisions which you are unable to alter or influence. You must then act in a way which conflicts with your firm ideas of what should be done. This conflict can quickly lead to disappointment and disillusionment, two potent sources of negative stress.

Furthermore, because you enjoy challenges, you may find yourself being asked to take on an increasing number of taxing and time-consuming projects.

Managing Your Stress

Learn to say no tactfully but firmly when your stress levels start to rise. Pay attention to your feelings and don't be afraid to express your emotions openly and honestly. Remember that what seems only logical to you may appear cold and heartless to less analytical thinkers.

Work Category Creators
Personality Symbol Circles

Your sensitivity makes it especially difficult for you to tolerate the unfair treatment of others. It is especially upsetting for you to observe such injustices without your being in a position to set matters right. You are also likely to find disciplining or directing subordinates stressful.

Managing Your Stress

Avoid being drawn into too many battles on the part of others, since these conflicts deplete your own ability to resist stress. Never feel too guilty if, despite your best efforts, you are obliged to let people down. Try to become more detached and objective in your professional dealings.

Work Category Creators *Personality Symbol* Squiggles

The disappointment and frustration which arise when your colleagues, superiors, or subordinates fail to share your enthusiasm for an idea can be a major source of stress. You may also risk investing energy in so many different activities that you make yourself more vulnerable to stress.

Managing Your Stress

If your enthusiasms are not receiving adequate outlets and encouragement at your present workplace, seriously consider finding a company which would value these qualities more highly. Smaller, progressive firms are often more receptive than larger, more conservative organizations. If such a change is impossible, have hobbies and leisure activities in which your energy and enthusiasm can find a rewarding outlet.

Work Category Communicators *Personality Symbol* Triangle

Because you are strongly goal directed, you run the risk of setting yourself unrealistic targets and then becoming stressed when you are unable to achieve them. Any such failure is likely to make you upset and self-critical.

Managing Your Stress

Try to be more philosophical in your approach to life. Learn to regard setbacks as valuable learning experiences rather than a reflection of personal inadequacy.

Work Category Communicators *Personality Symbol* Squares

A possible source of your stress is trying to cope with the highly subjective approach many people bring to a transaction. When this leads to a rejection of your well-reasoned arguments, you often feel disillusioned, resentful, or frustrated.

Managing Your Stress

Remember that logic often plays a very minor role in major decisions like the purchase of a house. Try to be as flexible as possible in your approach to clients, superiors, and subordinates.

Communicate with *Squares* on the basis of facts, with *Squiggles* enthusiastically, with *Circles* on human values, and with *Triangles* in terms of their life goals.

Work Category Communicators *Personality Symbol* Circles

Your intuition, empathy, and ability to relate to others makes you well suited to all kinds of selling, but you need to be satisfied that your customers are being fairly treated. If you work for a company whose business practices strike you as unfair, the conflicts aroused will generate significant levels of stress. You will also become stressed when you must disappoint people because of circumstances beyond your control.

Managing Your Stress

Try to work for a company that appreciates the importance of good employee relations and for an employer that is sensitive to human feelings. At the same time, develop a more objective approach to life.

Work Category Communicators
Personality Symbol Squiggles

You invest so much enthusiasm and energy in your career that rejection proves extremely stressful. Unlike *Triangles,* who become stressed when their goals are frustrated, your stress arises from having too strong an emotional commitment to each task.

Managing Your Stress

Avoid investing all your energy and enthusiasm in any one activity or task, especially if it is not fully appreciated by those you work for or with. Develop a variety of interests.

10

Creating a Stress Barometer

Creating a stress barometer offers a rapid way to keep an eye on your fluctuating stress levels. You can use it every day to check that you are neither rising nor falling from your PPSL.

Constructing Your Barometer

Make your barometer when you feel confident and relaxed, when you feel you are at your Peak Performance Stress Level.

Take two sheets of plain airmail-weight paper and place a sheet of carbon paper between them. With a ballpoint pen, write a half-dozen words across the top of the paper. Apply the amount of pressure you would normally use if writing a letter to a friend. Beside this line write PPSL.

Repeat the same sentence at the top of the page. This time apply the lightest pressure needed to produce a copy on the lower sheet of paper.

Write the sentence a third time at the bottom of the sheet. Use the heaviest pressure possible without tearing the paper.

Repeat the sentence a fourth time, midway between your

top (lightest pressure) and middle (PPSL) lines. Apply pressure halfway between your lightest and normal stroke. Beside this line, write the word "Retreat."

Finally, write the sentence between the middle (PPSL) and bottom (heaviest) lines, applying a pressure midway between your normal and heaviest stroke. Beside this line, write the word "Attack."

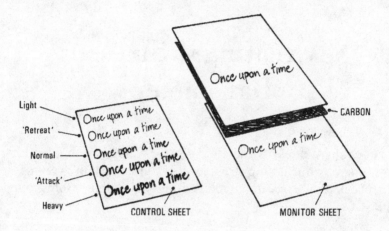

Light — Once upon a time
'Retreat' — Once upon a time
Normal — Once upon a time
'Attack' — Once upon a time
Heavy — Once upon a time
CONTROL SHEET

Once upon a time
CARBON
Once upon a time
MONITOR SHEET

Discard the top sheet of paper and use the carbon copy as your stress barometer. Its greater contrast makes for easier use.

To monitor your changing levels of stress, take two sheets of paper with a sheet of carbon between them, as you did when constructing your barometer. Write the test sentence applying normal pressure.

Compare the most recent version with your original. If the pressure applied is the same as the line marked PPSL, your stress is unlikely to have changed much. If the writing pressure has become lighter, closer to the line on your barometer labeled "Retreat," your stress level is falling below your PPSL. You may be understressed.

If the line is heavier than your PPSL, so that it more closely matches the line labeled "Attack" on your barometer, your stress level is rising.

Less stress is likely to produce a retreat from some challenging situations because your motivation has declined.

Increased stress suggests a more aggressive approach as you strive to maintain standards despite a less effective performance.

11

Testing for Negative Emotions

If you experience any intense negative emotion, for even a short period, your mind and body rapidly become fatigued. Anger and fear, emotions associated with the primitive fight-or-flight survival mechanism, cause the heart rate to speed. So, too, does unhappiness, even though it is not linked to the high muscle activity found during the fight-or-flight response. As a result, unhappiness is an extremely stressful emotion. Even pretending to feel an emotion, as actors and actresses do, is stressful. Research has shown that just putting on a sad expression causes the heart to speed up. In every case, you are making a significant withdrawal from your Stress Resistance Currency and running the risk of shifting away from your Peak Performance Stress Level.

Obviously, it is very useful to identify negative emotions. This may sound simple, but often we are not sufficiently in touch with our feelings to know exactly what it is that causes even a profound mood shift. We each have what I term our "Red Buttons," things we see, hear, or are compelled to do, which trigger a powerful emotional reaction. One of the hazards of an intimate relationship is that we quickly become aware of our partner's Red Buttons. Having identified them, it's then all too easy to punch in a required emotion. You want guilt, this anecdote never fails to arouse his guilty feelings. You want remorse, that comment always makes her remorseful.

If you sometimes feel worried, anxious, upset, or negatively aroused without really understanding why, here is a simple but effective way of testing which various remarks and comments might be responsible. It enables you to identify sources of stress operating below the level of conscious awareness.

Testing Negative Feelings

Stretch out your right arm (if right handed, left arm if left handed) and ask someone to push downward while you resist the pressure.

Now bring to mind any person, situation, activity, or challenge which you believe may be creating excessive stress. If you have any negative feelings, your arm will be unable to resist the downward force and will start to descend. If the emotion is positive, however, you will be able to continue resisting their pressure.

In this way you can monitor your reactions to *any* potentially stressful action, even though you are not aware it is causing— or is likely to cause—difficulties. Similarly, by focusing your mind on a positive idea, you will strengthen your arm's resistance to the downward pressure.

Naturally, you can test only two or three different thoughts in the same session, or normal muscle fatigue will cause your arm to droop. But, after allowing a few moments for recovery, you can repeat the test.

Why does this test work?

Understand that every thought, good or bad, constructive or destructive, produces a physical effect. So does every sound, sight, taste, and touch.

A relaxing image, such as a peaceful country scene, reduces

arousal, lowers blood pressure, and produces electrical patterns in the brain associated with calm. In contrast, looking at a bustling urban landscape increases arousal.

These responses happen within a few hundredths of a second, normally without our even being aware of what is happening. You can test the subtle interaction between mind and body, thought and action, with the following experiment:

Draw a circle on a sheet of plain paper. Now construct a small pendulum by attaching a weight to a piece of thread about 7 inches long. The weight should be heavy enough to keep the thread taut and allow it to swing easily in any direction.

Hold your hand steady above the circle, with the tip of your homemade pendulum around the center.

Concentrate hard on the idea that the pendulum will start swinging in a clockwise direction. Focus on this thought, strongly but keep your hand as steady as possible.

After a few moments, despite the fact that your hand appears not to have moved by even a fraction of an inch, the pendulum will start moving clockwise around the circle. Once started, it will gradually pick up speed until the initial, fairly tentative movement has become a clear and unmistakable oscillation.

Now focus on the thought that the pendulum should move counterclockwise. Sure enough, it will hesitate, oscillate uncertainly for a while, then start moving in the required direction.

There is nothing mystical or magical about any of this, although some people may try to persuade you that there is. All that is happening is that your concentrated thought is being transformed into muscle movements so slight and subtle as to be imperceptible to the naked eye. But, when amplified by the length of thread, they are sufficient to produce the desired movement.

The message is clear.

Negative thoughts will always cause you harm even though nobody else is aware of them.

Destructive ideas do not have to be translated into action to do damage. The thinker always suffers.

Silently snarl "I hate you" or "I'd like to kill you," and it's your own system which becomes the first victim of that mental poison.

Positive thoughts exert exactly the opposite effect. They lower stress, strengthen the immune system, and generate a health-enhancing state of mind and body.

12

Keeping Stress on a String

To use stress creatively, you must develop greater day-by-day awareness of especially stressful situations. This allows you to anticipate your own Red Buttons, which I described in the preceding chapter and which automatically trigger a sharp increase in your stress level. Only in this way can you prevent sudden surges in stress.

Besides identifying stressful situations, you must also become aware of how you felt, thought, and reacted. The most common method for doing this is keeping a stress diary. Such a diary, together with instruction for completing it, is in this book's appendix. Your stress diary can provide you with useful insights into your daily stresses.

If you find that keeping a stress diary is just one more chore in an already stressful day, here is a sixty-second alternative.

Take a piece of string about 8 inches long. Every time something stressful occurs, tie a knot in your string.

That's all you have to do.

Mark one end of the string in some way, such as with a drop of ink.

For stressful situations during the morning, tie knots toward the start of the string. For stresses later in the day, tie knots farther and farther along the string.

If you experience a major stress, tie two or three knots in the same place.

For example, suppose you are delayed by morning rush-hour traffic while driving to an important meeting. Your heart starts to race wildly as you worry about missing the appointment. You feel your hands sweating on the wheel. You silently curse the driver ahead, although you realize that losing your temper won't help. The next time your car slows to a halt, tie a knot at the beginning of your string.

At 11.30 A.M. you become involved in a dispute with a colleague and feel yourself getting tense. Tie a knot closest to the middle of your string.

In the early afternoon, you call on an important client who keeps you waiting twenty minutes. As you sit in the reception area, your anger at the impolite treatment and worry over all the jobs still to be done back at the office causes your stress level to rise sharply. Tie two knots.

In the late afternoon, a mountain of unexpected paperwork is dumped on your desk. It's all urgent! Tie a knot toward the end of your string.

Just before going to bed, examine your stress string.

Count the knots. Reflect on each. Assign each one a value in Stress Resistance Currency. Count the knots and add up the cost.

Each knot helps you remember not only what happened, but how you responded to that situation.

What you thought.

What you said.

The way your body responded.

How you felt after the event.

Consider whether, during the period that your stress existed, you were above or below your PPSL.

Spend no more than sixty seconds considering each knot. What could you have said differently—either out loud or silently—that would have reduced your stress or made it less painful to cope with?

What might you have done differently?

Find a better physical and/or emotional response and make up your mind to respond that way in the future.

13

Wrestling Alligators without Getting Eaten Alive

A therapist friend once remarked to me that while some of us have more alligators than others to wrestle with in life, and some are better at alligator wrestling, there comes a time in everybody's life when even the best wrestlers are at risk of being eaten alive. She meant events so highly stressful that we are overwhelmed, if only in the short term. Situations capable of creating such stress include bereavement, the diagnosis of serious illness, being fired, and discovering that your partner has been unfaithful.

The element common to each of these very different situations is that your control over events is lost. But even in these extreme circumstances, you can avoid being eaten alive by stress if you are able to adopt the correct attitude.

Changing Your Mind about Stress

In 60 A.D. the Roman philosopher Epictetus remarked: "Man is disturbed not by things but the views he takes of them."

Shakespeare echoed these sentiments by having Hamlet say: "There is nothing either good or bad, but thinking makes it so."

In a similar vein, Alexander Pope wrote: "All seems infected th' infected spy/As all looks yellow to the jaundiced eye."

Alfred Adler, an early disciple of Freud, wrote: "It is very obvious that we are influenced not by 'facts' but by our interpretation of them."

George Kelly, an influential psychologist, believed that events were meaningful only to the extent that they were seen that way by each individual. He wrote: "Reality does not reveal itself to us directly, but rather it is open to as many alternative ways of construing it as we ourselves invent . . . all our present perceptions are open to question and reconsideration . . . even the most obvious occurrences of everyday life might appear utterly transformed if we were inventive enough to construe them differently." As George Kelly expressed it, events do not carry their meanings "engraved on their backs," but have their significance imposed on them by the way different individuals interpret them.

Writers, poets, philosophers, psychologists, and great thinkers down the ages have asserted the essential truth of this statement:

Stress arises from an interaction between yourself and the situation in which you find yourself.

It is *your* perception of events, rather than the events themselves, which can cause your stress to rise above or fall below your Peak Performance Level.

A couple of case histories from my files will illustrate.

The Stress That Impoverished Nicky . . .

When 33-year-old Nicky was abruptly fired from a brokerage house, her stress levels soared and stayed chronically high.

"I felt so deeply ashamed, I cut myself off from all my old friends," she told me. "I wallowed in depression and self-pity, constantly reminding myself what a failure I was."

As a result of her negative self-talk, Nicky's confidence plummeted. She came to see herself as a loser.

After being unemployed for only three months, Nicky accepted a job with lower status, lower salary, and fewer prospects than her previous job, largely because she had convinced herself she was unworthy of anything better.

. . . *Enriched John*

Contrast this response with that of John, aged 32, after he lost his job at the investment bank where he had worked for ten years.

"At first I was devastated. The whole ritual of clearing my desk into a black plastic bag and being escorted from the premises by Security was horrible. I felt deeply ashamed and humiliated.

"But that black mood lasted only a few days. Then I managed to view my situation in a more positive light, to see what had happened as an opportunity instead of as a threat to my future success."

Because of his positive perspective, John's stress quickly returned to his Peak Performance Level. Calmly and optimistically, he reviewed all his options and developed a realistic plan to recover control over events.

"I decided to become an independent financial consultant. Although the going was tough, I never lost faith in myself."

Within twelve months, John had built a considerable reputation and a list of blue-chip clients, among which was the very bank which had fired him the previous year.

Two similar situations which provoked very different responses. For John, the stress of being fired became a spur to make positive changes in his life. For Nicky, excessive stress, fueled by self-blame and negative thinking, swiftly spiraled into chronic distress, with catastrophic consequences.

It's the same with insufficient stress. When 19-year-old Martin decided to study psychology at college, he didn't realize that statistics would form an essential part of his course. "I hated math in school and was totally bored by it," he told me. "At first statistics class was a dreadful bore. I could never bring myself to tackle the course work or study the lecture notes. My professor warned me I was heading for a failing grade."

Then Martin was fortunate enough to have an inspirational teacher who transformed his perception of statistics. "I suddenly started to see it as interesting, stimulating, and even fun. My motivation to study soared, and I began getting good grades, which encouraged me still further."

All that had changed was Martin's *perception* of statistics from being boring to being a compelling subject. As a result, his stress was raised to the optimum level for that subject.

Half-full or Half-empty?

Glance at the picture on the next page. Is the glass half-empty or half-full?

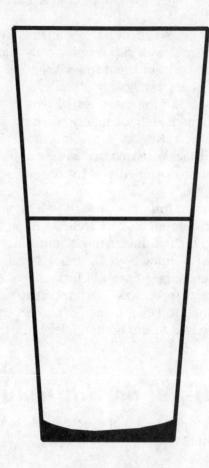

If your outlook is mainly optimistic, chances are you considered it half-full. If you tend to take a more pessimistic view,
you probably saw it as half-empty.

Optimism-Pessimism and Health

Because a pessimistic attitude is stressful, looking on the
dark side will undermine your mental and physical health.

Optimism, in contrast, promotes your well-being and is life
enhancing.

In one study, 100 healthy young men were divided into pessimists and optimists on the basis of their responses to a questionnaire. Their medical condition was then monitored over the next two decades.

By the age of 45, a majority of pessimists were displaying signs of chronic diseases, including heart attacks and arthritis.

Optimists suffered far fewer of these health problems.

Another project videotaped interviews with 122 Californian men who had suffered heart attacks were used to categorize them as either pessimists or optimists. Eight years later, 15 of the 16 most pessimistic men had died while only 5 of the most optimistic men had done so.

This study indicates that high levels of stress, associated with a pessimistic outlook, may weaken resistance to disease.

Dr. Judith Rodin, a Yale social psychologist, studied forty people aged between 62 and 85 with no diseases or physical conditions which might have adversely affected their immune systems. They were interviewed on several occasions over a two-year period, and their blood was analyzed for T-cell levels, a measure of immune-system strength. A significant relationship was found between those who showed a pessimistic outlook and those who had impaired immune function.

The Role of Positive Pessimism

These findings don't mean that pessimism has no place to play in life. When used appropriately, pessimism can help you reduce stress and avoid what could prove costly mistakes, since pessimists are often able to confront reality more clearly and directly than optimists. When the price of failure could be substantial, such as deciding whether to say or do something which might destroy a valued relationship, it's a good strategy to switch into pessimistic thinking to consider the worst possible outcomes.

Explaining Success and Failure

Professor Martin Seligman, of the University of Pennsylvania, coined the phrase "learned optimism" to describe how some people explain what happens to them in life. Pessimists blame bad things, such as marriage difficulties or job loss, on problems which are pervasive, enduring, and their own fault. Optimists view the causes of failure as *limited* to that specific situation, short-term, and due to circumstances beyond their control. These differences are crucial in your determining how much stress you will suffer.

Mark, aged 29, placed a very pessimistic interpretation on his failure to impress a promotions board. "Just another disappointment in a lifetime of failure," was his gloomy conclusion. "I'll never succeed because I lack the talent to get ahead." This explanation was *pervasive* ("another disappointment"), *enduring* ("I'll never succeed"), and *self-blamed* ("I lack the talent").

Mary, a self-assured 27-year-old, came up with an entirely different explanation for her poor showing at a job interview at which she arrived late because her car broke down. "I messed up this time, but it won't happen again," she said confidently. "I've learned important lessons which will ensure that I do better next time."

Her explanation was *limited* to that specific event ("I messed up this time"), *short-term* ("It's not going to happen again"), and *due to something beyond her direct control.* Finally, she saw her poor showing as a *learning experience* which would help her do better the next time.

Pessimism and Irrational Thinking

When things go wrong, if you offer yourself explanations which involve more than that specific situation, blame yourself, and see your failure as part of a continuing saga of set-backs, your attitude is pessimistic and your stress levels will remain high. When something goes right, you'll probably switch explanations. Now your success is specific, due to external causes, and is only temporary.

After he'd passed a graduate-school examination with higher-than-expected grades, Tony, aged 29, told me: "It was a fluke (specific). The paper must have been really easy (external). There's no way I can ever be so lucky again (temporary)."

Much stress is caused by pessimism, which arises from these ten most frequently reported, irrational thoughts.

How often do you fall into any of these self-talk traps?

1. All-or-nothing Thinking:

You assume: "Either I succeed at everything I attempt, or I am a complete failure."

Remember, the only way to learn is by making mistakes. In fact, if a job's worth doing, it's worth doing badly!

The only way we ever get anywhere in life is by building on the foundations of past errors. That's how as a child you learned the most basic lessons of walking, talking, and making sense of the world.

Labeling is an extreme form of all-or-nothing thinking. Here you hang a label around your neck on the basis of a few mistakes, or even a single mistake. "I failed, therefore I must be an all-time loser."

2. Filtered Thinking:

Involves focusing on mistakes while either ignoring successes entirely or insisting that they "don't count."

3. Overgeneralized Thinking:

You look on a single event as part of a pattern of inadequacy. "Because this relationship has failed, it must mean that I am incapable of ever sustaining an intimate relationship with anybody."

4. Mind-reading Thinking:

You assume that somebody thinks badly of you, without any evidence to support such a belief.

5. Fortune-telling Thinking:

You predict that things will turn out badly before ever making an attempt.

6. Magnification Thinking:

You exaggerate your problems and shortcomings.

The opposite is Minification Thinking, in which you greatly diminish or dismiss as insignificant the value of benefits and rewards. This is sometimes called "binocular" thinking, since events look either larger or smaller than they really are, depending on which end of the glasses are used.

7. Emotional Thinking:

Insisting that your negative self-talk offers an objective assessment of the way things really are. For example: "I feel guilty, so I must be a bad person."

8. "Should" Thinking:

You believe that things should always be the way you hoped or expected them to be. "I should feel this . . ." or "I should expect that . . ."

9. Personalization Thinking:

Holding yourself personally responsible for events which aren't under your control.

10. Social-expectations Thinking:

You assume that people must behave toward you in a certain way if you are to enjoy self-respect. Common examples are:

I expect others always to . . .

- · Treat me fairly
- · Keep their promises
- · Look on me as special
- · Reward my hard work
- · Tell me the truth
- · Recognize and appreciate my talents
- · Show me gratitude when I am kind to them
- · Love me as much as I love them

Because all these are absolutes, they generate far greater stress than such realistic expectations as: "It would be nice if people always treated me fairly, but I can't expect this will happen any more than they can assume that I shall always treat them fairly."

To control failure stress and ensure that fresh challenges are tackled with a positive attitude, you must avoid negative self-talk and counter irrational thoughts by finding realistic but optimistic explanations for what actually happens.

14

Coping with the Stress of Change

Although the causes of stress in modern life are extremely varied, two of the most significant shifts away from PPSL are caused by confronting change and dealing with time pressures. In this chapter, we will explore ways of dealing with change. Then, in the next chapter, I will describe practical ways for you to manage your time more efficiently.

Life Events and Change

As the pioneering work of Thomas Holmes and Richard Rahe shows, major life events, such as relocation, the ending of an important relationship, serious illness of a loved one, children leaving home, losing your job or retiring and, above all, bereavement all involve significant increases in stress.

The death of a loved one is especially stressful because bereavement is the most powerful emotion most people ever experience. While there are no simple, speedy ways of resolving such stress, there are some practical suggestions to make the loss easier to bear.

Show Your Emotions

Never feel embarrassed about being emotional. Expressing your feelings openly acts as an emotional safety valve.

Chemical analysis of the tears shed by people experiencing a strong emotion shows they are significantly different from tears produced physically, by peeling onions. This difference leads some psychologists to conclude that crying removes stressful chemicals and restores the body's chemical balance.

It is undoubtedly true that a good cry helps you feel better. In one study, 85 percent of women and 75 percent of men said crying had a positive effect on their mood.

In another study, a group of healthy men and women were compared with others, of similar age and background, suffering from stress-related disorders. The main difference found between these two groups was that the stress sufferers considered tears a sign of weakness or loss of control. As a result, they struggled to remain dry eyed, however harrowing their experiences, feeling ashamed if they ever did cry.

The healthy people saw crying as natural and normal. They felt no embarrassment over shedding tears. Other studies found that widows who weep after their husbands died were less likely to suffer stress-related illness than those unable or unwilling to grieve openly.

Time Will Heal

It is normal—and essential—to pass through recognized stages of grieving.

The first stage is denial. An instinctive reaction to bad news is to gasp, "Oh, no . . ."

The second stage is guilt, as you reproach yourself with such thoughts as "If only I had behaved differently, this might never have happened!"

Following closely comes anger directed toward the other person: "How could he cause me such pain?"

Do not feel bad about these emotions. They are a natural part of the grieving process. They must be worked through before you can come to terms with your loss. Always allow yourself the time to mourn.

Once the first shock has passed, however, it is essential to stop brooding about what might have been and to start searching for any good features in the change. While these may be almost impossibly hard to identify, there is usually at least a glimmer of hope in even the most tragic circumstances.

Review any options which have been opened up to you by the change in terms of your overall goals in life and seek to replace what has been lost by activities which offer some level of stimulation and gratification, even if it is very different. For example, a new widow or widower might spend more time with grandchildren and derive some pleasure by telling them stories or teaching them new skills.

Talk to Friends

Numerous studies have confirmed that support and comfort from family and friends are powerful antidotes to excessive stress. A nine-year-long study in California showed that people with close friends not only have a happier but a longer life. They run less risk of becoming depressed and recover faster from surgery or a heart attack. Another study focused on 109 people living close to the Three Mile Island nuclear plant in Pennsylvania, which suffered a radiation disaster in 1979.

Researchers found that those who received little or no support from neighbors, family, and friends suffered the greatest number of stress-related problems even though the levels of stress hormones in their blood were no higher than other residents.

So talk about your problems, fears, and feelings. Confide in those closest to you.

But Never Sacrifice Your Independence

Once the worst of your crisis is over, take prompt action to reduce excessive dependency on friends and family and reassert responsibility for your own life. Only in this way can you regain control over events and rebuild lost confidence and self-esteem.

The Stress of Career Changes

Not surprisingly, job changes are most stressful to ambitious men and women whose work is often central to self-identity and esteem.

The key to controlling the stress generated by this type of life event lies in planning.

Anticipating Change

While some kinds of stress occur so unexpectedly that no anticipation and planning prove possible, many life events can be predicted well in advance. Children grow up and leave home. One day we must retire from full-time work.

Instead of allowing retirement to creep up on you almost unaware, prepare well in advance for all the changes this will bring about. Start as early as possible because time has a habit of slipping past with remarkable speed, and today is the tomorrow you failed to prepare for yesterday!

Create a Life Plan

Anticipation and preparation become far easier to manage if you have some overall plan for your life. This doesn't have to be—indeed should not be—engraved in stone. But it needs to be sufficiently clearly stated to provide you with a guide through the alligator-strewn swamps of an uncertain future.

The starting point for creating such a plan is to establish your life goals, those things you intend to accomplish in terms of your family, social life, career, and leisure pursuits.

An effective if somewhat macabre method for deciding on your life goals is to prepare your own ideal obituary! You can do this by completing the form below. Don't respond as if your life were going to end tomorrow, but when, where, and how you would ideally wish it to draw to a close. Write down not your present accomplishments, however considerable, but your ambitions still waiting to be fulfilled.

_____ died last night aged ___ in _____
  (Your name)   (Where you would

_____ _____ worked as a _____
most enjoy living.)   (Your name)   (the career you'd like to

_____ achieving the position of _____. Outside
follow)   (How high you hope to rise)

his/her work _____ 's chief interests were _____
                       (Your name)   (The hob-

_____. _____
bies, leisure activities, interests you have or would like to follow)   (Your

_____ 's many achievements included _____
name)   (What you have

_____. He/She will be best remembered for
or hope to accomplish)

_____.
    (All you have or would wish to achieve)

This fantasy obituary will help you identify your major goals in life.

Having done that, it is easier to work out the practical steps which must be taken if your goals are to be achieved.

Here's an example of a fantasy obituary completed by one of my clients:

> Peter died last night aged <u>110 and in perfect health right up to the end</u> in <u>his luxurious home on a romantic Pacific island.</u> <u>Peter</u> worked as a <u>consultant,</u> achieving the position of <u>CEO of his own company.</u> Outside his work <u>Peter's</u> chief interests were <u>his wife and children, with whom he had a warm relationship.</u> His hobbies included <u>SCUBA diving, sailing, and swimming.</u> <u>Peter's</u> many achievements included <u>giving generously to charity and helping to support many worthwhile causes.</u> He will be best remembered for <u>his friendship, generosity, and good company.</u>

Having written your obituary, ask yourself what you are doing to turn those dreams into reality.

Peter decided to take more active steps to protect his health by being careful about his diet, getting more exercise, and becoming less hostile. He took a correspondence course to develop new management skills, spent more time with his family, and took up SCUBA diving.

Ask yourself:

Where would I like to be, and what do I hope to have achieved . . .

In the next twelve months (short-term goals)

In the next two to five years (medium-term goals)

Five or more years from now (long-term goals)

Establishing goals and preparing a plan, which anticipates and prepares for inevitable change, enables you to avoid considerable stress.

By safeguarding your Stress Resistance Currency in this way, you will have more in reserve to deal with life's unavoidable and unexpected stresses.

15

Three-D Time Management

How often do you feel excessively stressed by any of these situations?

- Having too little time during the day to finish all your work projects?
- The feeling that time is passing far too rapidly and without your achieving your key goals in life?
- Not spending enough time with your family or friends?
- The speed with which time seems to be passing?

If you found yourself sharing some or all of those difficulties, you could be in need of more effective time management.

What Goes Wrong

Philip G. Zimbardo of Stanford University speculates that the way we use time reveals something about our mental and physical health. In a study with Dr. Alexander Gonzalez, chairman of the psychology department at California State University, Zimbardo identified a number of different Time Zones into which people can become locked. Relating these to my own stress research, the most significant Zones seem to be:

Zone One—Present-Fatalistic: There is little or no sense of urgency. Even when things don't get done on time, people in this Zone are seldom overly concerned. They often move and talk slowly, dislike deadlines, and find it hard to be punctual. Not surprisingly time stress is seldom a problem.

Zone Two—Present-Hedonistic: People in this Zone are impulsive, dislike planning, make decisions on the spur of the moment. These people have some time-related stress because they exhaust themselves by being constantly on the go.

Zone Three—Future Oriented: People in this Zone are constantly looking to the future rather than dwelling in the present. They buy life insurance, plan their days, weeks, or months in advance, and take deadlines very seriously. They experience a moderate level of time-related stress.

Zone Four—Time-Press: This Zone is largely inhabited by people like George, my workaholic client whom we met in Chapter 1, and other Type-A personalities. People in this Zone set challenging deadlines and are preoccupied with getting things done on time. Unsurprisingly, they are the most affected by time stress.

Which Zone Do You Occupy?

The test at the start of this book, where I asked you to judge the passing of 60 seconds, helps to identify whether time stress is a problem for you.

Repeat that test now, using the more detailed analysis below:

Glance at your watch, then close your eyes. Sit still until you judge that 60 seconds have passed.

Open your eyes and check.

Time elapsed: 30 seconds or less. You are likely to be in the Time-Press Zone and find this source of stress a significant problem.

Time elapsed: 30 to 50 seconds. You are under a fair amount of time stress and may have difficulty satisfying conflicting demands for your time.

Time elapsed: 51–60+ seconds. Your approach to life is sufficiently relaxed to make it unlikely that time stress is much of a problem.

The Perception of Time

When many changes are taking place around us, time speeds up. The higher your stress, the faster it speeds past. Examination takers know only too well that the shortest time span in the world is the last five minutes at the end of an exam!

When bored, apathetic, and insufficiently motivated, our time sense slows. The lower our level of arousal, the more tediously time seems to pass.

You can also change the perception of time through hypnosis. In one experiment, Milton H. Erikson and Linn F. Cooper used hypnosis to stretch out time to such effect that for one subject 10 seconds felt like 23 minutes.

The secret of coping with a hectic schedule is to allow yourself recovery periods between bouts of high arousal. These need not be lengthy. A recuperation period lasting no more than one minute can restore your Peak Performance Stress Level.

Later in this book you will find ways to recoup your energy by using special breathing, relaxation, and massage techniques.

Stress and Time Management

While efficient time management will help you find a few more hours in the week, it will not reduce your stress by any significant amount. The newly found time will be filled instantly with other tasks, some of which may be more stressful than those dumped.

Suppose you decide to stop reading junk mail to make time for preparing an extra report per week. Spending a few moments each day idly glancing through brochures and mail-order offers might have been quite relaxing, whereas producing another report might be rather stressful.

Therefore, although I will provide some ideas for using time efficiently, the major way of reducing time stress will be to change your *perception* of time.

What to Do

Step One—Start Making More Time for Yourself

Start by setting major goals in the key areas of Family, Social, Career, and Leisure. Then it becomes possible to assign priorities to various activities according to their relevance in enabling you achieve those goals. As a result, you will find it far easier to respond appropriately to various demands on your time.

When faced with any task, there are only four possible options.

You can Drop It, Delay It, Delegate It, or Do It.

Drop It—This sounds easy, but breaking established habits of time wasting often requires determination and self-discipline. Check for time-wasting habits in your routine. Before carrying out any activity, ask yourself: "Will this help me achieve a goal in life?" If the answer is no, then there is little point in investing even a few minutes of your life in carrying it out.

Delay It—Negative delay, or procrastination, involves replacing a high-priority activity with one of much lower priority. You know you should be preparing a difficult report, but instead you squander your time on the very low-priority task of straightening your desk. This avoidance tactic only increases stress at a later time.

Positive delay is involved when . . .

· You postpone a low-priority task for one with a high priority.
· You put off a task which, by pressing a Red Button, arouses powerful and disruptive emotions such as anger, depression, bitterness, or envy.
· You have insufficient information or the requisite amount of skill to undertake the task efficiently.
· Your physical or mental state is such that it seems unlikely you could carry out the job successfully.

Delegate It—Effective delegation is one of the greatest time-stress savers there is. Not only does effective delegation enable you to assign more time to tasks which only *you* can perform, it usually means that a better job is done by everyone.

Do It—This is the stage where many people come unglued. Although they have clearly identified a high-priority job, they can never find the right moment to begin.

As a final chore, spend a minute each evening planning your schedule for the following day. Set aside time for routine tasks and those you simply can't avoid. If possible, begin with the more demanding tasks and leave the easier ones until later in the day. That way you'll be investing your energy more efficiently. Your plan must be sufficiently flexible to cope with the unexpected.

The unscheduled meeting, an unexpected visit from a major client, the surprise party invitation, that last-minute panic to meet a sudden rush deadline and so on. This is where setting yourself clearly defined goals proves especially helpful. Since you are obliged to handle the unexpected or to cope in an emergency, it becomes far easier to decide which of your other commitments can best be Dropped, Delayed or Delegated.

Three tests for time well spent.

Was the task *Necessary*—not just nice but necessary? Don't get into the habit of doing things simply because they were useful in the past.

Appropriate—is the task something you should be doing or delegating?

Efficient—is there a better, faster, more time-effective way of doing it?

Step Two—Learn to Switch Your Time Zones

Identify your more frequent Time Zone from the descriptions above. Now practice changing gears by moving between them. If, for instance, you prefer to plan well ahead, a Zone Three characteristic, move into Zone Four by acting on the spur of the moment now and again. Behave spontaneously from time to time, by making an impetuous decision or altering your routine impulsively.

Similarly, if you favor an unplanned approach, start scheduling some activities more precisely. Move from Zone Four to Zone One by not allowing yourself to be so pressured by time. Adopt an occasional *mañana* outlook. This is especially important if you deliberately put yourself under time pressures, by setting needlessly tight deadlines, for example. When making appointments, allow more leeway for delay, by saying, "I'll be with you around nine-thirty tomorrow morning," instead of specifying, "I'll see you at nine-thirty," which imposes an often unnecessary time stress.

Step Three—Create a Time Stretcher

While you are in a relaxed state (see Chapter 24) visualize someplace which is special to you. Spend 60 seconds in there, silently repeating: "All time is now. I have all the time I need for productive dreams."

After a minute, open your eyes. You'll feel not only more relaxed but also refreshed by the change of pace.

Step Four—Slow Time with a Yo-yo

For some, this suggestion will seem too silly to be worthy of serious consideration. However, so many of my clients have reported good results from slowing time in this way that you could well benefit from giving it a try.

Buy a yo-yo in a bright, cheerful color. Find one which is well balanced and moves smoothly. Whenever you feel time-pressure stress building up, play calmly with your yo-yo for 60 seconds.

Focus on the movement of the yo-yo and practice making it rise and fall as slowly as possible. Use the yo-yo to wind down after each period of hectic activity.

This tactic seems to work for three reasons. First, it focuses concentration on something outside yourself, thus providing a distraction from circular worries. Second, the rhythmic action is mentally soothing and may even assist the logical left and intuitive right sides of the brain to integrate more efficiently. Finally, the childlike aspects of "playing" with a toy can be both comforting and reassuring at times of stress. It liberates you from the constraints of the adult world, re-creating a period of your life when it was possible to forget everything by playing.

16

Coming Up When You Are Down: The Power of Positive Self-Talk

Here are six of the worst confidence destroyers which my clients have identified. If any are familiar, they may be a significant source of excessive stress in your own life.

· Failure to attain important goals
· Inability to achieve a desired performance
· Rejection by a loved one
· Stupid mistakes or bad decisions at work
· Disappointments and setbacks
· Not living up to the expectations of others

These all serve as potent sources of negative self-talk. They give rise to confidence-destroying, circular thoughts which bring you farther and farther down. They may prevent you from tackling activities you'd really love to do, which could be a source of considerable satisfaction and enjoyment. By doing so, they lower your level of stimulation below that required for Peak Performance.

Equally, they may trigger high levels of anxiety as you anticipate and dread the seemingly inevitable pain and humiliation of failure, either in your own eyes or in those whose opinions you respect.

What to Do

Step One—Tune in to Your Negative Self-talk

At random times during the day, pause and ask: "What am I telling myself about myself right now?" Regular monitoring is important because it's all too easy to slip into a habit of negative thoughts. Your automatic response to a setback can become: "I'll never cope with this . . ." "How could I be so stupid . . ." and so on.

Every negative idea has at least two stressful consequences. First, it undermines self-esteem, making you less capable of performing successfully. In a very short while, a confidence-zapping self-fulfilling prophecy of failure is established. Second, it depletes your limited reserves of Stress Resistance Currency, without any positive return.

There are two occasions in which negative self-talk is highly likely and especially damaging.

· Immediately before a significant challenge
· Immediately after an unexpected setback

In both cases, the powerful emotions of anxiety, anger, frustration or disappointment, make it ever harder to review the situation calmly and rationally. At such times it is especially important to reflect on what is about to happen—or has just occurred—as objectively as possible. The best way of doing so is to step outside yourself.

Try to imagine you are viewing events through the eyes of a trusted—but not directly involved—third party, such as a friend or colleague. Consider how things are likely to appear to them.

Ask yourself: "What would he/she tell me under these circumstance?"

Step Two—Analyze Your Explanations

Have you fallen into any of the traps described in the previous chapter?

If any of the irrational thoughts listed in the last chapter are familiar, jot them down on a card and carry it with you. The next time your monitoring picks up a negative statement or idea, identify the type of thinking behind it. Consider whether there is a realistic alternative explanation for what happened.

One of my clients found he was far more likely to make mistakes in the morning than during the afternoon. He was one of those people whose natural biological rhythms mean they are more alert later rather than earlier in the day. When he recognized this pattern, he switched his routine tasks to the morning and saved major decisions for after lunch.

Step Three—Defend Yourself

When unfairly criticized by others, we are usually quick to defend ourselves. But if the criticism comes from within, accusations are more likely to stay unchallenged.

If somebody said, "You are stupid," you'd probably rebut their claim with vehemence and offer examples of the many occasions when you had acted in a highly intelligent manner. Yet if you tell yourself "I am stupid," you will probably passively accept this damaging and unreasonable assessment.

Allowed to go unchallenged, negative self-talk quickly destroys self-esteem and assurance.

Whenever you detect a negative thought or statement, counter it at once by a realistic comment. For example, following a silly mistake, you say to yourself, "What a stupid person I am!" From now on, respond with a spirited "So I made a mistake. That doesn't mean I'm incompetent. Most of the time

I enjoy great success. So let's review what happened to see where I went right as well as what I did wrong."

Carrying out this positive analysis in no more than one minute as an immediate, gut reaction helps to avoid unhelpful brooding on the setback. It also makes it easier for you to challenge negative self-talk on a regular basis. Get into the habit of finding an optimistic explanation for even the most depressing failure. It will keep you motivated and enthusiastic, rapidly reducing your stress to Peak Performance Levels.

17

Coping with the Stress of Criticism

Business joke: There are two types of criticism. *Destructive* criticism is where people say you're an idiot; *constructive* criticism is where they explain exactly *why* you're an idiot!

Unfortunately, a large number of managers and executives appear to believe that these are their only options when criticizing. As a result, they send stress levels soaring while utterly failing to correct the very problems their comments were intended to highlight.

Some people are far more vulnerable to criticism than others. The first step is to decide whether criticism is a significant source of stress for you.

Test Your Reactions to Criticism

Score statements from 1 through to 5, where 1 = Very True and 5 = Not True at All. I . . .

Become upset when criticized
Lack confidence
Rely on the views of others

Dislike unfamiliar challenges
Need constant reassurance from those around me
Look for approval from superiors
Feel very upset by failure
Am unsure of myself in new situations

Scoring:
8–15: You are very vulnerable to criticism and at risk of becoming highly stressed, even when those comments are deserved and could help you learn important lessons.
16–30: You can handle reasonable criticism without difficulty, but may still become overly stressed by unfair or unreasonable comments.
30+: Criticism probably pours off you like water from a duck's back. While this makes excessive stress less likely, it could also mean that you take insufficient notice of important criticism, and thereby fail to avoid similar mistakes in the future.

While you can't do much to change a critical boss or carping partner, there is a great deal you can do to reduce the effects on your levels of stress.

Remember that buying a criticism means spending precious Stress Resistance Currency. If valid and helpful, the criticism might be worthwhile purchasing because it will provide a learning experience.

When undeserved, unhelpful, and downright destructive, there's no point in squandering your SRC reserves. Here's how to decide whether or not to buy criticism.

What to Do

The next time you feel stressed by criticism, whether at work or at home, jot down the remark on a piece of paper small enough to fit into the palm of your hand, with fingers spread.

Now ask yourself *five* questions.

1. Is the critic worthy of my respect?

The answer depends on whether he or she has made the criticism from a position of superior knowledge, skill, or experience. In other words, do they really *know* what they are talking about?

If a qualified instructor criticizes your driving, he or she probably does deserve respect. But if somebody lacking any special driving qualifications does the same, he or she almost certainly does not.

Where no superior expertise exists, fold your little finger down over the paper. Now ask

2. Is the criticism reasonable?

Was it expressed in a way designed to point out and improve your performance, or was it merely an excuse to launch a personal attack?

Was it stated calmly and coherently, or blurted out in a rage which took the remarks to an extreme?

Was it intended to be helpful or hurtful?

If you can fairly consider it unreasonable, fold your next finger down over the paper. Now ask

3. Is the criticism realistic?

After a traffic accident made him late for work, Peter's boss criticized him sharply for unpunctuality. "He refused to even hear my explanation," Peter recalls. "It was most unfair since my timekeeping is good." Anytime you are blamed for something beyond your control, regard the criticism as unrealistic and fold down your middle finger. Now ask

4. Is the criticism relevant?

Critical comments intended to hurt or humiliate are rarely relevant. The critic launches an attack which has got nothing to do with the issue in hand.

After she had incorrectly collated an important report, Mary's line manager launched a furious assault on her physical appearance, claiming that she took insufficient care over her grooming. Clearly this attack was designed to make her feel bad, rather than point out and correct the error.

If you can honestly say that a criticism is irrelevant, fold down your index finger. Finally ask yourself

5. Is the criticism rational?

Is it a fair and objective appraisal of *all* the relevant information?

Irrational criticism is often motivated by envy, jealousy, or ignorance. Such comments usually say more about the critic's problems than about your own alleged mistakes.

If judged irrational, fold your thumb over the paper, crumple it up, toss it away, and forget the criticism. The comments are clearly not worth further time or effort.

Destroying a criticism in this way helps banish painful emotions.

Imagine your stress being discarded into the garbage with the ball of crumpled paper.

But suppose not all the fingers can be folded down because you have to agree that your critic's views should be respected, or that the remarks were reasonable, realistic, relevant, or rational? The very fact of reaching such a conclusion makes the criticism helpful and constructive.

Reflect on how you might do or say things differently to avoid such criticisms in the future. At the same time, reduce your stress by taking the following steps.

Step One—Accentuate the Positive

When reflecting on the criticism, use the PIN approach. This stands for *Positive*/*Interesting*/*Negative*.

Start by considering all the *P*ositive features of the criticism. Next think about anything *I*nteresting which was said, whether positive or not. Only then should you dwell on the *N*egative aspects of the situation. And even here you must review the event in a constructive manner.

Avoid falling into the "Yes, but . . ." trap. "Yes, but I've always done it this way."

Even when such objections are valid, raising them in your

defense inhibits further consideration of whether you could learn from that negative comment.

Change "Yes, but . . ." to "Yes, and . . ." Say to yourself, "Yes, and I could change this . . ."

Even the most unwelcome and hurtful criticism can contain at least one positive feature. By finding and focusing on it, you achieve two important benefits.

First, you make it more likely that something good can come out of an apparent setback. Second, you ensure that the other person will be more receptive to your response.

Step Two—Evaluate the Situation Objectively

Once all the positive aspects have been considered, seek out any Red Buttons triggered by their comments.

We all have Red Buttons: comments, remarks, accusations, charges which have the power to trigger an emotional reaction out of all proportion to the actual criticism. Once our Red Button has been punched, it can arouse such powerful feelings of anger, panic, outrage, guilt, jealousy, despair, and envy we are no longer capable of thinking straight or forming rational judgments.

Never act on a criticism in such a disturbed emotional condition, but postpone further internal consideration until you have calmed down.

Step Three—See It as Criticizing the Performance, Not the Performer.

Even when we know a criticism is justified, it can cause such distress that we defend ourselves by switching off mentally, avoiding the issue or refusing to acknowledge the comment was justified. By doing so, we fail to learn the lessons necessary for avoiding similar mistakes in the future. If you feel stressed and angry, calm down physically by using one of the Sixty-Second Relaxation or Breathing-Control techniques described in later chapters.

Then, when you feel calmer, take another minute to reflect

on the criticism. Only this time view it as a comment of what was done, rather than taking it personally.

If your critic was angry or upset, consider which of his or her Red Buttons you might have pressed to provoke such a powerful reaction.

Such insights can help you avoid a similar situation in future. They might give you a winning edge in subsequent negotiations, since your critic has betrayed a potentially vulnerable spot in his or her makeup.

18

Beating Worry Stress

Worrying is a significant cause of stress for a great many people. Even those who appear confident and relaxed may still be making themselves miserable by worries. Worries can take the form of disturbing thoughts which circle endlessly or pop unbidden into your mind—typically during the early hours of the morning—making you feel anxious depressed and uncertain.

There are three main types of worry.

Acute Worries

Come unexpectedly and unbidden to mind, perhaps as a result of something you've seen or heard which trigger a chain of negative associations, initially below the level of consciousness.

By the time you become aware of them, the stress generated can be so overwhelming that it leads to what has been termed "awfulizing": making a major problem out of a minor difficulty by carrying worry to absurd extremes.

Chronic Worries

Are never far from your thoughts no matter how busy and distracted you can keep yourself. They cast a pall of gloom over everything you do, however enjoyable those activities used to be.

When severe, they result in a condition known as *anhedonia,* an inability to find pleasure in anything. Anhedonia is a symptom of depression.

When Worry Strikes

You are most vulnerable to both chronic and acute worrying in the hours before dawn. Napoleon once remarked he had "yet to meet an officer with three-o'clock-in-the-morning courage."

The cause is biological rather than psychological. Around this period of the day, physical resistance is at its ebb. Temperature and blood glucose levels are low, the metabolism sluggish. Dangerously sick patients are more likely to die at this time than at any other.

Not surprisingly, your bodily state exerts a considerable influence over your mood. Worries about health, money, career, or relationships chase uselessly about your head, driving sleep ever farther away.

Remember: Worry Solves Nothing

Most sensible people recognize that worrying is completely unproductive. Now researchers at Columbia University have proved it. They showed:

- 40 percent of what we worry about never happens
- 30 percent of the problems are over and done with by the time we start to worry
- 12 percent of our worries are about nonexistent health problems
- 10 percent of worries are actually centered on the wrong things

Which leaves just 8 percent of worries worth bothering about. No single approach to bringing worry stress under control is likely to work on its own. Experiment with the following, in conjunction with the rapid relaxation, positive mental imagery, and breathing techniques described later in this book.

What to Do

This procedure is divided into ten practical steps. Use as many of them as necessary to help you control worry stress.

Step One—Become More Objective about Your Worries

Identify the 8 percent of reasonable worries by spending 60 seconds carrying out this mental checklist. Keep an eye on your watch and strictly ration yourself to 15 seconds per answer. Ask yourself:

1. How likely is it that this worry will happen?
Rate the likelihood on a scale of 1 = Extremely improbable to 5 = Virtually certain.
2. How accurate is my information?
Rate accuracy of your information from 1 = Highly dubious to 5 = Absolutely reliable.
3. Are there practical steps which might prevent it?
Rate your coping capacity between 1 = I know a great many practical steps to take and 5 = I see absolutely no way of improving matters.

4. How serious are the consequences?

Rate from 1 = Hardly serious at all to 5 = Catastrophic. Your score.

5–10. The worry is too trivial to bother with.

16–20. The problem is so intractable that there is nothing you can do to influence what happens. *Stop worrying.*

11–15. Worrying is reasonable but not sensible. Take practical steps to resolve the situation by . . .

· Improving your knowledge of the subject

· Developing a strategy for avoiding or lessening the consequences of what is happening

In addition, try one of more of these 60-second procedures.

Step Two—Absurdly Exaggerate Your Worries

Paradoxically, taking the worry to an absurd length will often make it easier to deal with.

For example, stuck in traffic on your way to an important appointment with a bad-tempered client, you start worrying over his likely anger. Instead of brooding, take your worry to extremes.

Imagine the client growing so furious that he attacks you with a double-bladed battle-ax the moment you enter his office. Imagine him chopping and slashing through the furnishings as you duck and weave your way around their office.

Picture the client red-faced with fury, growing devil horns in rage. See him foaming at the mouth, his eyes bulging from his head.

Fantasize about the receptionist pulling a lever and opening a trapdoor which drops you into a pit full of alligators, as she yells "Thus perish all unpunctuals."

The more ridiculous you can make the image, the more effective it will be in diffusing your anxiety and stress. Keep developing this fantastic imagery for a full 60 seconds, by which time your worry should seem utterly absurd.

Step Three—Become More Philosophical about Your Worries

Follow the advice given to World War II fighter pilots: "When flying, one of two things can happen. Either the flight will be uneventful or something will go wrong. If the flight is uneventful, there is no cause to worry. If something goes wrong, one of two things will happen. You will either crash or you won't.

"If you do not crash, there is no need to worry. If you do crash, one of two things will happen. You will either live or die. If you live, there's no cause to worry. If you die, you won't be able to worry—so why waste time worrying?"

Step Four—Count the Cost of Your Worries

Work out the price that has to be paid for every worry in Stress Resistance Currency. Since you are certainly not getting value for money, the next time a worry arises, point out to yourself that the cost is far too high.

Step Five—Erect a Mental Barrier to Your Worries

Whenever a worry pops into your mind, train yourself to immediately think *yellow unicorns.* Focus on these mythical beasts for 30 seconds, picturing them as vividly as possible in your mind's eye.

Since you can hold only one thought in conscious awareness at a time, focusing your mind on a totally different topic—and one which is most unlikely to arouse any worrying associations —blocks that worry instantly.

Now distract yourself by turning your attention to some mentally challenging task.

Step Six—Use Distractions

Switch your attention to a task which is pleasurable and demands concentration.

Spend 60 seconds thinking about an enjoyable activity you've planned for later in the day.

Step Seven—Delay Unavoidable Worrying

Practice "Just In Time Worrying." When a worry rated 11 to 15 arises, tell yourself: "I am right to feel concerned. But as nothing bad can happen for twelve hours, that's when I'll start worrying."

Step Eight—Identify Irrational Idea Worrying

Some of our worst worries stem from irrational thinking.

Here are a dozen of the most potent sources of needless worry. Although widely believed, each statement is quite untrue. If any of these ideas forms the basis of a chronic worry for you, try to recognize it for the myth which it is. From now on, when the idea comes to you, tell yourself that the thought is as untrue and unhelpful as believing the world to be flat or the moon made of green cheese.

#1 I must be approved of and loved by everybody I know: family, friends, and even casual acquaintances.
#2 I must be unfailingly competent and exactly perfect in all I do.
#3 It is terrible if things, people, or events are not as I wish them to be.
#4 I must have somebody or something stronger or greater than myself to rely on.
#5 I am helpless and cannot control what I experience or feel.
#6 Good relationships depend on selflessness.
#7 People will reject me unless I continually please them.
#8 If people disapprove of me, it means I must be wrong or bad.
#9 Being alone is negative. My happiness, pleasure, and fulfillment can occur only through other people.
#10 There is a perfect love and perfect relationship somewhere to be found.

#11 My value as a person depends on how much I achieve.
#12 The answer to all my problems is out there somewhere.

Step Nine—Prevent Early-morning Worrying

Whenever possible, exercise before going to bed. People who work with their brains all day may feel intellectually exhausted without being physically tired. A brisk walk, jog, swim, or aerobic session during the evening helps ensure a full night's rest. And while asleep, you won't be worrying.

Avoid drinking coffee or smoking just before going to bed since they stimulate the system and make deep sleep less likely.

While an alcoholic nightcap helps some people sleep, avoid too much strong drink because it interferes with natural sleep patterns.

Keep your bedroom cool and well ventilated, with your bed snug and warm.

Drink a glass of warm milk before bed. This contains the amino acid L-Tryptophan, which stimulates the production of serotonin, a neurotransmitter involved in sleeping. If making such a drink is too much of a chore, or you don't want to wake your partner, prepare a Thermos bottle earlier in the evening.

If you can't sleep, get out of bed and spend 60 seconds scribbling down brief notes about any worrying thought that is circulating in your mind. Return to bed. If you are still awake and worrying 10 minutes later, repeat the exercise. Continue until you fall asleep again. It is essential to get out of bed before writing your worries down in order to break the habit of waking up and worrying. Writing worries down, a process known as "externalizing," makes them easier to consider objectively.

Recall a time in the past when you felt extremely sleepy but had to fight off rest because of external demands, perhaps while driving long distance, when cramming for an exam or listening to a dull after-dinner speech by your boss. Concentrate on this image and you will start to feel drowsy. Now disregard rational demands and tell yourself something like: "Never mind about arriving at my destination on time—I must stop and take a nap" or "I don't care if my boss does see me, I'm going to snooze." You will gradually find yourself drifting off to sleep.

Reassure yourself that early-morning worries have little or no bearing on reality. They relate mainly to low levels of blood glucose.

Focus on interesting, pleasurable activities scheduled for later in the day. This aids relaxation and encourages sleep.

Step Ten—Send Your Worries Up in Smoke

To prevent bringing work worries home, send them up in smoke, either literally or symbolically. If possible, write your chief worries on scrap paper, then burn it. Tell yourself those concerns have been turned to smoke and ashes and need not be resurrected until tomorrow. If those worries are unreasonable, their cremation should be regarded as putting an end of to them. Where you can't physically burn your worrier, use the procedures described in Chapter 24 to develop a relaxed mental state. Now imagine your worries going up in smoke and disappearing from sight, at least until you return to work the next day.

19

Controlling Stress by Controlling Breath

We breathe some 16,000 to 20,000 times a day, and every breath contains about 10 sextillion atoms—10 followed by 22 zeros! Every time you inhale, therefore, you take into your lungs one atom from every breath ever breathed by the whole of mankind. Since this action is repeated daily by some 4 billion people, it has been calculated that each breath contains 10^{15} atoms breathed by every other person on earth within the last few weeks and more than a million atoms breathed personally, at some time, by every person who has ever lived—including Buddha and Christ.

Some 3,000 years ago, mystics claimed that "life is in the breath," by which they meant far more than just lungs, blood, circulation, and the exchange of gases. They meant that life energy the ancient Indian language of Sanskrit calls *prana*.

Breath is the vehicle for *prana*.

When your breathing is inhibited and inefficient, your life force is diminished, and stress quickly rises above your PPSL.

When your breathing is full and efficient, your whole system —emotionally, physically, and intellectually—is enhanced. That is why we describe somebody filled with creative life energy as being "inspired" or having an "inspiration."

Breathing and Changing

Everything in the universe is in a constant state of change. Your stomach lining renews itself within one week, your skin within a month, your liver every six weeks. In five years, not a single atom of your present body will be here, and five years ago the you of today did not even exist.

Certain elements in your body, such as the phosphorus in your bones, were formed at an earlier stage in the evolution of our galaxy. Like many elements in the earth's crust it was cycled through a lifetime of several stars before appearing on earth and finding its way into your body.

There is a constant biodance, a persistent equilibrium, an endless exchange of elements between living things and the earth.

We are part of a basic oneness with the universe. Breathing is the vital link in this equilibrium.

Stress Control Means Breath Control

One of the first things which happens when we become stressed is that our rate and type of breathing changes. It may even cease momentarily.

If you held your breath when clenching your fist in the test at the start of this book, your response to any sudden stress is likely to be a held breath.

Your breathing may increase from a normal rate of between 12 and 16 breathes per minute. It may also become shallower, so that only the upper portions of your lungs are used. Rapid, shallow, breathing is called *hyperventilation* and occurs invariably during panic attacks.

How Breath Change Affects Your Body

The range and variety of distressing effects caused by changes in breathing are seldom fully appreciated. They include racing heart, chest pains, dizziness and faintness (especially in young people), anxiety, panic, an inability to concentrate, diminished mental and physical performance, disturbed sleep, nightmares, increased sweating beneath the arms and on palms (emotional sweating), a feeling of unreality, visual disturbance, and even hallucinations.

In people who are vulnerable to hyperventilation, it is possible to provoke a full-blown panic attack merely by asking them to breathe rapidly and shallowly for a couple of minutes.

The Medical Consequences of Hyperventilation

All these damaging effects are due to faulty breathing, which creates an imbalance in the ratio of carbon dioxide to oxygen in our blood.

As is well known, we draw in oxygen from the outside air when inhaling and expel carbon dioxide, the waste product of metabolism, with each exhaled breath. These gases travel around the body in our bloodstream in a very tightly controlled balance.

By reducing levels of carbon dioxide in the arterial blood, hyperventilation creates a condition known as *hypocarbia*, in which the very small carbon dioxide molecules are able to pass in and out of nerve cells (neurones) even faster than water. Even minor hypocarbia causes an immediate migration of carbon dioxide from the neurones. This triggers an increase in nerve-cell activity and electrical discharge in the associated nerve fibers. At the same time, veins constrict, reducing oxygen supplies to the brain and creating sensations of dizziness, faintness, and unreality. One widely used first-aid treatment for panic is to breathe into and out of a paper bag. By rebreathing carbon dioxide-rich exhaled air, the balance is restored and panic abates.

Stress-related hyperventilation triggers a vicious cycle in which rapid breathing produces distressing physical symptoms, and the anxiety these arouse creates a further increase in stress.

Holding your breath in response to stress leads to a rapid buildup of carbon dioxide and produces equally distressing mental and physical consequences.

But these are not the only stress problems associated with faulty breathing. Attached to your ribcage is the diaphragm, a domed sheet of muscle which acts as a flexible wall dividing the abdominal and chest cavities. Your diaphragm plays an important role in digestion and circulation by preventing stomach acid flowing back into the esophagus and aiding the heart in pumping blood up from the legs, abdomen, and pelvis.

When the diaphragm flattens and contracts during deep breathing, abdominal pressure increases. Together with the abdominal muscles, this creates an inflatable "jacket" which helps support the lower back. A well-functioning diaphragm is able to make a significant contribution to your health, enabling you to combat stress more effectively. An inefficient diaphragm depletes reserves of SRC by undermining your physical well-being.

How Do You Breathe?

Carry out this 60-second examination the next time you are stripped to the waist.

Looking into a mirror, study your chest carefully while continuing to breathe normally. Notice which parts of your chest rise and fall with each complete breath.

Now place your hands on your breastbone, one above the other.

Inhale slowly and deeply.

Exhale.

What type of movement did you see and feel?

Did your upper or lower hand rise farthest?

Keeping one hand on your breastbone, place the other against your back, reaching as far down between your shoulder blades as possible.

Inhale slowly and deeply once again. Exhale.

Did you see and feel most movement in the upper or lower portion of your chest?

Finally, place a hand low down on either side of your chest.

Inhale deeply as before. Exhale.

Where is movement most noticeable this time, in the upper part of your chest, revealing shallow breathing, or down toward your abdomen, indicating deep breathing? In distance, the difference may amount to only inches. Physiologically and psychologically, it makes a very great deal of difference.

Deep and Shallow Breathing

We can breathe in one of two main ways.

The first is by raising the chest wall using the intercostal muscles between each rib.

The second method is to flatten and contract our diaphragm, while moving the upper ribs and breastbone forward and upward to increase chest capacity.

In each case, a partial vacuum is created in the chest cavity, which draws air into the lungs.

If your ribcage moved mainly outward and upward, your breathing is costal.

If most of the work was done by your diaphragm and muscles forming the abdominal wall, your breathing is deep and diaphragmatic.

The Penalties of Shallow Breathing

Except when exercising vigorously, costal breathing is inefficient because most of the air reaches only the middle areas of your lungs rather than the lower portions which are richest in oxygen-absorbing blood vessels. Because of this, your body must work harder to achieve the required level of gas exchange. Since your oxygen requirement depends on how hard your muscles are working, costal breathing requires a greater number of breaths per minute than deep, abdominal breathing. This faster, shallower breathing increases the risk of hyperventilation during stressful encounters.

To make matters worse, costal breathing is part of the primitive fight-or-flight response, a mechanism which evolved tens of thousands of years ago, when all the dangers faced were physical and the only survival options were to fight or flee.

This subconscious association means that simply by using costal breathing, stress levels increase sharply.

Deep or diaphragmatic breathing, by contrast, infuses the blood with additional oxygen and causes the body to release mood-enhancing endorphins. Because expansion and ventilation occur in the lower parts of the lung, which are richest in blood vessels, deep breathing is also more efficient. We can slow down our breathing and still achieve the optimum exchange of gases. Since we breathe in this way when we feel calm and composed, simply switching to diaphragmatic breathing reduces tension and creates a feeling of composure.

Check Your Breathing Regularly

Monitor your breathing several times each day in a variety of situations, such as immediately on waking, after commuting through congested traffic, during lunch, prior to a challenging meeting, and while working at your desk.

This checking will help you become aware of the way different situations affect your breathing. If you find you are constantly using shallow, costal breathing, get into the habit of breathing more slowly and deeply. You will find practical exercises for deep breathing later in the book.

20

Preventing Muscle Stress

Try this simple experiment.

With your eyes closed and arms outstretched, try touching the first finger of each hand.

Most people are able to do this without difficulty because sensors within every muscle provide the brain with information about its position in space and how much strain it is under. A muscle under needless tension is sending a constant stream of stressful messages to the brain.

When muscles contract, their blood vessels are constricted and blood flow decreases. This leads to a buildup of such waste products as carbon dioxide and lactic acid, while denying the muscles oxygen. The result is yet more distress.

Muscle Spasm

On occasion, a group of muscle fibers contracts suddenly, producing a painful muscle spasm. Unless treated, the spasm produces knots of hard, tangled lumps known as trigger points, which limit movement and can be extremely tender to the touch. Having once occurred, spasms are more likely to happen again, causing chronic discomfort.

Treating Muscle Spasm

For a muscle in spasm, cold is far more comforting than heat, so use an ice pack made by wrapping cubes or crushed ice in a towel, to protect the skin from frostbite. Cold numbs the nerves, reducing the pain signals which are causing blood vessels to contract. These vessels can then dilate, increasing blood flow to the affected muscles. Cold also diminishes the buildup of fluid in the muscle, another source of pain. Keep the pack on for 20 minutes, off for 20 minutes, for several hours. After 48 hours, change the cold compress for a warm one.

You may also benefit from massaging the painful area for 5 to 10 minutes. I explain how later in this chapter.

Posture, Pain, and Muscle Stress

Faulty posture, caused by sitting hunched over a desk or computer terminal for lengthy periods, can also lead to cramping and eventual muscle fatigue. A diet low in calcium can also aggravate the situation.

Unfortunately, tension signals from affected muscles are often ignored until the pain becomes so distressing that it compels us to pay attention to what is happening.

Analyzing Your Muscle Awareness

The following exercises, which take about 5 minutes to complete, will help you get in touch with your body. The results also direct you to the best techniques for reducing or removing any stress-induced discomfort before it can cause serious trouble.

How to Score

Every exercise which you are able to perform without stiffness, discomfort, or undue effort scores 0.

If the exercise cannot be done at all, either because your muscles were too stiff or the movement proved painful, score it as 10 points. Between these extremes, award yourself points depending on how easy or hard you find a particular exercise.

If you are in the slightest doubt about your fitness to tackle this analysis, have high blood pressure, or recently underwent major surgery, seek advice from your doctor before attempting the test.

You will need a pillow and a quiet place where you can lie full length on the floor. Loosen tight clothing and remove your shoes before starting.

One—*Neck:* Look first to the left, then to the right, turning your head as far as possible without discomfort. Notice whether it was harder to turn your head in one direction than the other.

Two—*Neck:* Tilt your head forward and rotate in a full circle, first clockwise then counterclockwise. Try bringing your head as close to your shoulders as possible, in order to really stretch the muscles.

Three—*Shoulders:* Standing upright, try to reach behind your shoulder with one hand and up your back with the other, touching your fingers. If unable to touch your fingers, check in the mirror to see how far apart they are.

Four—*Upper back:* Lie face-down with a pillow under your stomach and hands at your sides. Try lifting your upper back and shoulders, without any help from your arms, keeping the lower part of your body flat on the floor. This time award yourself 0 points if you can keep yourself raised for 10 seconds, 5 points for 5 seconds, and 10 points for anything less.

Five—*Lower back:* Remove the pillow and place your hands, palms upwards, beneath your thighs. Keeping your legs straight, raise them as high as possible and count how long it is possible to hold them in this position without effort or pain. Score as for upper back.

Six—*Stomach:* Roll onto your back, still lying down, and place your hands behind your head. Raise your bent knees as high as possible, keeping your feet flat on the ground. Without moving your legs, try to touch your elbows to your knees. This time do not hold the position. Score on the basis of ease and comfort, with 0 points if it was performed effortlessly and 10 points if you could not do it at all.

Seven—*Wrists:* Stretch out each hand in turn and rotate your wrists, first clockwise then counterclockwise.

Eight—*Upper legs and knees:* Standing, place your feet 12 inches apart and attempt to place your palms on the floor between them.

Nine—*Lower legs:* Rise right up onto the balls of your feet and walk around the room, keeping your legs straight. Try to do this for 30 seconds. No score if this proved effortless, 5 points if you experienced twinges of discomfort after 15 seconds, 10 points if you were unable to do this for the full 30 seconds.

Ten—*Ankles:* Standing straight, rest the right hand on a chair or table for balance. While lifting the left leg as high as possible, rise onto the ball of your right foot. Hold for a slow count to three, then lower your left leg and come down on the right. Extend the left leg out to the side again, raising yourself onto the ball of the right foot. Hold for a count to 3 as before.

Finally, stretch the leg out behind your body. Repeat all three exercises with the right leg. Write in your scores on the chart below, or copy this page. Start working with the exercises linked to those analysis exercises which received the highest score.

Analysis	Body Part	Score	Exercise
One/Two	Neck		1
Three	Shoulder		2
Four/Five	Upper/lower back		3

Analysis	Body Part	Score	Exercise
Six	Stomach		4
Seven	Wrists		5
Eight	Upper legs/knees		6
Nine/Ten	Lower legs/ankles		7

Massaging Away Muscle Stress

Massage is one of the most powerful antidotes to physical distress and tension. The first thing a hurt child does is seek comfort by gently massaging the afflicted area.

When used in a more sophisticated manner, massage can do much more than ease pain. Your hands have the power to promote permanent well-being and to maintain stress at Peak Performance Level.

The secret lies in knowing exactly how and where to apply this healing touch. Ideally, you should have a regular massage, not only to soothe away tension, but as an aid to general health by stimulating blood flow and lymphatic drainage.

A full body massage from a qualified practitioner will take between 30 and 60 minutes. If you can do so, I strongly urge you to make a regular massage part of your stress-control program.

Even without professional assistance, the techniques described later in this book, all of which may be self-administered in a minute or less, will prove extremely useful in controlling stress.

The obvious difficulty with massaging yourself is that some of your muscles will be working and therefore still under tension. You can, however, easily and effectively massage specific parts of your body such as your face, scalp, neck, shoulders, hands, arms, lower back, calves, and feet.

The best time is while having a bath or before sleep. Although, ideally, you should massage the skin directly, it is still possible to produce good effect through light clothing.

Types of Massage

First let me explain the terms used to describe various forms of massage.

Effleurage is a French word meaning "to skim over." This technique involves a stroking motion which is firmer on the *upward* stroke (in the direction of the heart) than on the return. Effleurage can be performed with both hands simultaneously or one hand after the other.

Petrissage, another French word, means "to knead," and describes a movement performed by pressing the muscles firmly against the underlying bones using the palm of your hand. This can be done by one hand, using a continuous motion, or alternating hands.

Deep friction massage is performed by making small, circular movements using one or more fingers pressed firmly against the muscles. When rotating your fingers, it is important not to let them slide across the skin, which should move with your hand.

Preparing for Massage

When massaging away stress at home, apply some lubricating oils first. I will describe the most effective types to use for various forms of stress in the next chapter.

You will also find it helpful to create an aromatic soother, which is ideal for enhancing the power of self-massage. The soother is a ball of wax, scented with essential oils. Choose the oil most appropriate to your needs, as explained in the next chapter.

The Ingredients for Your Soother

You will need a cake of paraffin and some lavender oil, which can be obtained from any well-stocked health store or pharmacy.

Preparing the Soother

Place a small metal container in a large pan of water and bring to a boil. Melt the wax in the small container, adding 15 drops of lavender oil and stirring with a wooden spoon. Cool. When the wax is almost solid, remove and mold into balls about the size of your hand. For storage, wrap in aluminum foil and store in an airtight container.

Applied to aching or tense muscles, soothers have an effect similar to liniment, although they are considerably more relaxing. Soothers are especially helpful if you are stressed before or after strenuous physical activity, such as sports.

Preparing Your Hands

Before starting massage, always warm your hands by rubbing them together briskly, then shaking them as if drying off water. Oriental specialists claim this "charges" the hands with healing power, the left hand (Ying) being negative and the right (Yang) positive.

Where there is time, enhance your massage with the following warm-up exercise:

Lie on your back and stretch your arms over your head. Take a deep breath and, while exhaling, stretch your arms and legs. Inhale and relax. Repeat twice. If space permits, roll onto your right side, arms and legs stretched out in front. Lifting your left arm, circle slowly to the right side, allowing your left leg to follow the movement around.

Continue so that the gentle momentum rolls you onto your other side, bringing your right arm over to the new starting position. Repeat two or three times.

A Note of Caution

Massage is normally a safe and extremely beneficial method for reducing excessive stress. But there are a number of points to bear in mind.

Any persistent pain is a warning that something is not quite right with your body and should be taken seriously. Always consult your doctor about any chronic pain or one which causes you concern.

Seek medical guidance about self-massage if you are recovering from a serious illness, following surgery, or while you are running a fever.

If you are pregnant, you should not massage your abdomen or lower back. This is especially important in the early weeks of pregnancy, or if you have a history of miscarriages. This restriction also applies if you have had abdominal surgery.

When in any doubt, always seek the advice of your doctor.

21

Scents Which Banish Stress

"Odors act powerfully upon the nervous system," wrote the seventeenth-century author Johannes Muller. "They prepare it for all pleasurable sensations, they communicate to it that slight disturbance or commotion which appears as if inseparable from emotions of delight, all which may be accounted for by their exercising a special action upon those organs whence originated the most rapturous pleasure of which our nature is susceptible."

The value of scents was noted by Aristotle, three centuries before the birth of Christ, while among the Romans aromatic baths were a prelude to lovemaking, as were massages with sweet-smelling oils and the use of perfumes on the head, hair, body, and clothing. When, in the sixteenth century, Sheikh al-Nefzawi of Tunisia wrote one of the world's first sex manuals, it was not by chance that he titled it *The Perfumed Garden*.

There is evidence that the Egyptians practiced aromatherapy more than four thousand years ago. Certainly the power of scent to enhance physical health as well as mood has been known to Middle and Far Eastern medicine for thousands of years.

It is only fairly recently, however, that aromatherapy has come to be more widely accepted in the West.

Recently attention has been focused on the vomeronasal

organ, or VNO, located inside the mucous membrane which covers the plow-shaped septum, the cartilage dividing the nostrils. The name is derived from the Latin *vomer,* meaning plow.

Identified more than a century ago, the VNO was generally regarded a useless vestigial relic from our primitive past. Today, however, this tiny organ is considered by many researchers to be of considerable significance in our perception of scents, especially those which appear odorless to us. It seems to act as the receptor of a sensory system separate from smelling—almost literally a sixth sense. Neural pathways from the VNO travel directly to the hypothalamus, the part of the brain responsible for basic emotions and drives such as fear, anger, hunger, and sex, as well as regulating bodily functions such as temperature and heart rate.

Aromatherapy is based on the principle that scent can both heal the physical body and promote your emotional well-being. The therapeutic art involves the use of aromatic extracts from wild or cultivated plants, free from pesticides and gathered at full maturity. Some of these essences, which may be extracted by distillation, pressing, and maceration, may be inhaled. Others are used directly on the skin. A few drops sprinkled into your bath water will envelop you with soothing, stress-reducing fragrances.

Scents also act as powerful memory triggers. For many people, one whiff of sea air or countryside will evoke a whole host of pleasant, relaxing memories. Smelling antiseptics can increase stress by awakening memories of being in a hospital or back at school. Sniffing a subtle fragrance, such as almond, while conjuring up some happy memory, helps raise your spirits on a later occasion. The next time you feel upset or depressed, inhaling the same fragrance will bring the happy memory vividly back to mind, and will improve your mood.

For all these reasons, I have found essential oils invaluable in both rapid and long-term control of stress.

Preparing Essential Oils

For massage oils, use a dilution of three drops to two tea-spoonfuls (1/3 ounce) of carrier oil. If you want to make up a 3-ounce bottle, use 30 drops of your chosen essential oils.

The carrier oil serves as a vehicle for the blend of essences so they can be applied to the skin. Almond oil provides a skin-nourishing carrier.

Prevent Oxidation

Almost all vegetable and essential oils become rancid when they oxidize, producing an unpleasant odor in vegetable oils and a loss of freshness in the essential oils. As this process cannot be reversed, be sure to keep your oils in dark, airtight bottles, preferably well filled. A few drops of wheat-germ oil, which is rich in vitamin E, act as a natural antioxidant and can also be added. Sandalwood oil is the best fixative, although you can also use cedarwood. Fixatives make the scent last longer, so that the oil does not lose too much fragrance as it evaporates.

A good blend for stress is:

Basil 1 drop
Geranium 2 drops
Lavender 2 drops

For inhalations, add 8 to 12 drops to a bowl of hot water. For a facial steamer, add 4 to 6 drops to the hot water. For relaxing bathing, add between 3 and 5 drops of essential oil to your bath water.

Essential oils should be used with discretion since they have a powerful effect. With the exception of lavender, which is excellent for treating spots or blemishes, no essential oil should be applied directly to the skin.

When blending, fill your bottle with the carrier oil or oils, and then add the essences by drops. Cap the bottle and shake it gently.

Oils for Controlling Stress

There are a great many different essential oils, and it's worthwhile experimenting to find those most personally beneficial in controlling stress. Here are eight which I have found most helpful with a wide range of clients:

#1 Bergamot:

The rind of a fruit, resembling a pear-shaped orange, which grows in Italy, it must not to be confused with bergamot or bee balm found in North America. Named after the city of Bergamo in Lombardy, bergamot is used to scent the popular Earl Grey tea. Stimulating, uplifting, antiseptic, and antidepressant, it is excellent for treating general anxiety. Do not apply to the skin before going out into sunshine or exposing yourself to other sources of UV light.

#2 Camomile:

Gentle, relaxing, and soothing, this is one of the oldest-known medicinal herbs. With an applelike fragrance, it was called *kamai melon*—ground-apple—by the Greeks. The type most commonly used as camomile tea is known as German camomile.

#3 Clary sage:

Warm and euphoric, this oil induces a sense of well-being. The plant resembles common sage, but its blue flowers are smaller. The name *clary* is derived from the Latin *sclarea*, meaning clear. A native of Syria, France, Italy, and Switzerland, this plant was used in ancient times. A clear oil with a sweet, slightly nutty flavor, clary sage blends well with lavender, juniper, and sandalwood.

Clary sage is an excellent general tonic and pick-me-up. In fact, a few drops in your bath can lead to a mild form of intoxication. It is also excellent for lifting depression.

#4 Lavender:

A relaxing antibacterial oil, it takes its name from the Latin *lavare,* to wash. Lavender was a favorite bath perfume among Romans. Although grown in all European countries, the main commercial producer is France. The scent, widely used in perfumes, is so familiar as to need no description. It is good for reducing panic and calming frayed nerves. Its antiseptic properties also make it invaluable for treating many skin problems including insect bites and stings, acne, boils, eczema, and dermatitis. Lavender oil can also be used to treat—but not prevent—sunburn. When used to treat muscle aches and pains, apply lavender in a concentration of 2 to 4 drops per 3 ounces of carrier oil. A lavender-scented bath last thing at night will help ensure deep and truly restful sleep.

#5 Melissa:

This lemon-scented herb is found in Europe, Middle Asia, and North America. Its leaves are small and serrated, the flowers white or yellow. The name comes from the Greek for "bee," an insect which is especially attracted to the plant.

The eighteenth-century herbalist Joseph Miller wrote: "It is good for all disorders of the head and nerves, cheers the heart, and cures the palpitation thereof, prevents fainting and melancholy. . . ." Melissa has a joyful effect on the spirit which is common to aromatic oils.

#6 Neroli:

Orange blossom is extracted from the white flowers of the bitter orange *(Citrus aurantium).* The name probably comes from the sixteenth-century Princess Anne-Marie of Nerola who first used it to perfume her gloves and bath water. Its most common use is in eau de Cologne where it blends with lavender, lemon, bergamot, and rosemary to form the classic toilet water. Neroli is one of the most effective sedative/antidepressant oils and may be used for insomnia, anxiety, and depression.

#7 Peppermint:

Soothing, stimulating and refreshing peppermint was very popular among the Greeks, who used it to flavor wines and sauces, as well as in medicines. While the United States produces more peppermint oil than any other country, that cultivated in Italy, Japan, and Great Britain is generally considered of superior quality. Recent research has shown that peppermint is an excellent stimulant. One sniff is often all it takes to feel mentally and physically aroused. So potent is this effect that some Japanese companies now introduce occasional puffs of peppermint into the air conditioning to keep their employees alert. One company even provides a peppermint machine and instructs its salesmen to take a whiff before leaving to close a deal. They claim that selling has improved significantly since the device was introduced. Peppermint can also be used as a massage oil to combat muscle fatigue.

#8 Ylang-ylang:

This sensual, soothing, euphoric oil comes from the yellow flowers of a tree which grows 60 feet high and is cultivated in Java, Sumatra, and Madagascar. It must not be confused with the inferior "cananga oil." Ylang-ylang means "flower of flowers," and it has an exotic, very sweet scent reminiscent of jasmine and almond. Ylang-ylang lowers high blood pressure and relieves tachycardia (rapid heart rate) and hyperpnea (an abnormal increase in the rate and depth of breathing). It is excellent for combating anger and tension. However, the oil should not be used in concentrated amounts since it may then lead to headache and nausea.

These eight oils are only a tiny portion of the vast number of essential oils available for aromatherapy. If you are unfamiliar with this form of stress control, start using some of those listed above. But do experiment with other oils, since they have such a wide range of health-promoting properties.

22

Beating Start-the-day Stress

How you feel at the start of a new day depends, to a great extent, on both your general attitude toward life and how you treated your system the night before. Drinking too much alcohol, coffee, or eating spicy food may leave you sluggish and headachy. So, too, can a disturbed night's rest, caused perhaps by worries or anxieties.

I shall be describing ways of ensuring a more restful night's sleep in Chapter 29.

If you are depressed or bored by the prospect of what lies ahead, your mental and physical arousal will almost certainly be below Peak Performance level. If you are apprehensive of what the day holds and feel unequal to the challenges ahead, your level of arousal may be unhelpfully high.

Depression and lack of motivation cannot be resolved briefly or simply. In these circumstances, it is often sensible to reexamine your life goals and reassess your priorities as described in Chapter 14.

You may also wish to explore ways in which irrational thoughts and unrealistic expectations (see Chapter 13) might be responsible for your lack of enthusiasm and energy.

If you are significantly overstressed before the day even begins, then irrational thoughts and unreasonable expectations might also be at least partly to blame. You might also find it useful to examine ways in which you allocate and manage time for different tasks. One reason for excessive early spending of our Stress Resistance Currency is going almost directly from sleep to full wakefulness, leaping out of bed as soon as the alarm sounds—or racing to make up for time lost after unwisely allowing ourselves a few more minutes in bed. However pleasant it may be to snatch a little extra rest, you have to balance that enjoyment against the additional demands which running late is going to make on your reserves of SRC.

A more gentle return from sleep to full wakefulness, which allows sufficient time to carry out the techniques described below, is a far better preparation for the new day.

Assuming that your stress on waking is neither far too low nor excessively high, the Rapid Stress Control techniques described below will enable you to achieve the optimum level quickly and easily.

Your working day can start stressed before you even get out of bed. Here's how to start it alert and relaxed:

Technique #1

Before getting out of bed, starting with your right foot, bend your toes toward the instep. Inhale deeply. Hold for a moment, then curl the toes in toward the sole, breathing out at the same time.

Repeat three times, then do the same for the left foot.

Now lengthen your body in a long, languid movement like a big cat stirring lazily from sleep. Push down with your left foot to stretch the leg muscles, then repeat with your right foot.

Stretch each arm separately.

Get out of bed. Stand upright, with both feet placed firmly on the floor, and take two deep breaths.

Curl the toes of both feet inward while inhaling. Straighten and stretch them while exhaling.

Repeat three times.

Technique #2

Use this technique in the morning and whenever you experience

- Mental and physical fatigue
- Lethargy or lack of enthusiasm
- Sudden energy loss at any time of day

Breathe in Energy

Oxygen flowing into the body reenergizes every cell. Try to picture this happening while doing this exercise, which can be done sitting or standing. You may find it easier if you close your eyes.

If the air is fresh and clear, stand by an open window when performing this exercise.

Take a deep breath and feel your abdomen expanding as you bring your arms around in front of you and slowly up over your head.

Stretch slowly as your palms reach up toward the ceiling. Rock your body from side to side by shifting the weight between your right and left foot then back again.

As you inhale, imagine the clean, pure breath filling your body with light and energy, dissolving away stress and tension.

Breathe out while slowly bringing your arms down.

Repeat three times.

Focus on any area where you feel tension. Imagine the inhaled breath moving into this spot and dissolving away the stress. Picture your whole body filling with energy.

Use Clary Sage

If very fatigued on waking, add a few drops of this essential oil to warm—not hot—water and inhale deeply while splashing the water onto your face.

Energize Your Breakfast

Avoid a high-carbohydrate breakfast; it will make you sleepier.

Do not make do with several cups of strong coffee or tea, which produce excessive arousal. Try and start the day with fresh fruit and some protein.

Optimal performance and physical health depend on the efficient function of your adrenal glands. Unfortunately, stress leads to shrinking (atrophy) of this vital gland. Ensure optimal adrenal functioning by eating foods rich in potassium and low in sodium. Your daily potassium intake should be between 3 and 5 grams. Foodstuffs high in this vital mineral include:

FRUIT	Potassium (in milligrams)
Banana (1 medium)	440
Cantaloupe (1/4)	341
Dried apricots (1/4 cup)	318
Peach (1 medium)	308
Orange (1 medium)	263
Apple (1 medium)	182
FISH (per 3-ounce portion)	
Flounder	498
Salmon	378
Haddock	297

Take Ginseng

Ginseng, an ancient Chinese and Korean tonic, protects you from mental and physical fatigue while increasing your resistance to stress. Research shows it improves the ability to tolerate stressful surroundings, increases alertness, enhances performance, and boosts endurance. A dose of 25 to 50 mg. of ginsenoside—the active ingredient of ginseng—should be taken each day. With a high-quality root, take 1–2 grams daily in divided doses, which provides 20–40 mg. of ginsenosides. Alternatively, take a standardized extract which ensures greater control over quality and dosage.

Listen to Uplifting Music

Music has always been renowned for the powerful effect it has on our moods. Music is ideal for controlling stress, either lifting the spirits or helping you to relax more easily and fully.

Although the actual choice is very personal, many people find, for example, that Albinoni's *Adagio* brings tears to their eyes, Bruckner's *Ave Maria* sends a tingle down the spine, while Prokofiev's *Fifth Symphony* causes the heart to race. As a rule, unexpected changes in tempo make the heart race while melodic changes create a pleasurable shiver down the spine.

Create your own relaxation/wake-up/inspirational tape by rerecording favorite pieces on a special stress-control cassette. But remember that any such duplication may be an infringement of copyright.

One side is for Action. Choose brisk, arousing, music to boost your energy level and prepare yourself for challenges demanding vigorous action.

For the second, Calm Down, side of your cassette, select music which helps you feel more peaceful and relaxed. Flute, harp, piano, and string ensemble pieces are more soothing than vocal ones.

Always listen to soothing music while driving, since music with a fast, powerful beat encourages risk taking and speeding.

The ideal tempo for relaxation is slightly slower than your normal, resting, heart rate. Choose sonatas and symphonies played *adagio* (slow tempo) or *andante* (moderately slow). They will reduce your blood pressure and slow your heart, encouraging it to beat in time with the music. Classics meeting this requirement include:

Bach's *Brandenburg Concerto No. 4,* 2nd Movement
Bach's *Orchestral Suite No. 2* (Saraband)
Holst's *The Planets* (Venus)
Ravel's *Mother Goose Suite,* 1st Movement.

Suitable New Age music includes:

> Kitaro's *Silk Road* (Canyon Records)
> Steven Halpern's *Spectrum Suite* (Halpern Sounds)
> *Inside Paul Horn* (Golden Flute)
> Emerald Web's *Valley of the Birds* (Bobkat Productions)
> George Winston's *Autumn* (Windham Hill)

For many people, the most soothing sounds and music come from nature: gently flowing streams, birdsong, a breeze rustling leaves, waves lapping gently on the shore, and whale songs can all inspire a sense of tranquility and openness.

Listen only to music you like. If listening becomes a chore, the tape could become an additional source of irritation and stress.

If you notice your breathing becoming slower and deeper while listening, then the music is relaxing.

If you feel an increasing tension in your solar plexus or neck, the music is arousing you.

Far better to start your day listening to such a compilation than tuning into the news on television or radio. Most news will be bad, depressing, and generally stressful. For the most part, acquiring this knowledge is of absolutely no value to you —at least as an introduction to the day—and merely serves as an immediate debit on your SRC.

Summary of Technique #1

IN BED, BEND TOES TOWARD THE INSTEP.

INHALE DEEPLY. HOLD. CURL TOES TOWARD SOLE.

EXHALE.

REPEAT THREE TIMES. CHANGE FEET.

STRETCH LIKE A BIG CAT STIRRING FROM SLEEP.

PUSH DOWN LEFT FOOT. REPEAT WITH RIGHT FOOT.
STRETCH EACH ARM SEPARATELY.
STAND UPRIGHT. TAKE TWO DEEP BREATHS.
CURL TOES INWARD WHILE INHALING.
STRETCH THEM WHILE EXHALING.
REPEAT THREE TIMES.

Summary of Technique #2

STRETCH. INHALE. BRING YOUR ARMS OVER YOUR HEAD.
IMAGINE YOUR BODY FILLING WITH LIGHT AND ENERGY.
LOWER YOUR ARMS SLOWLY.
REPEAT THREE TIMES.

23

Combating Commuting Stress

For millions, the daily commute, often through rush-hour traffic or on congested public transportation, is a highly stressful and disagreeable experience. If your company offers flextime, use it to beat the rush by arriving earlier or later than the majority of commuters.

Where feasible, consider alternative transport. The best of all is to walk or cycle at least part of your journey. If you cycle through heavy traffic, however, a breathing mask is a useful safety precaution. But make sure it is clean. Recent research has shown that the masks worn by city cyclists are so dirty that they are a health hazard! At the end of your journey, take a few moments to destress yourself with these rapid-control techniques.

Technique #3

Take a deep breath.

While doing so, raise your shoulders gently, as though shrugging.

Hold for a moment, then breathe out as you release.

Spread out your fingers, stretch, and release.

Clench them into a fist and release.

Repeat three times.

Stretch your neck by turning your head from side to side and nodding. Do this slowly, allowing time for the muscles to stretch at the farthest limit of each movement.

Technique #4

Your neck is your body's crucial point of balance, so you should become conscious of its position at all times and take practical steps to reduce stressful activities.

While on the telephone, make certain to hold your head and neck upright. Sleep lying on your back with your head resting on a low pillow or rolled-up towel.

Traveling, whether by car or on public transportation, often means sitting so that your neck receives inadequate support. As a result, tension quickly develops in these muscles, leading to headaches and general discomfort.

Technique #5

This exercise increases your alertness by improving blood flow to the brain. In addition to combating travel stress, it will prove very helpful after periods of intense concentration.

When exercising your neck muscles, make sure that all the movements are smooth and gentle. Avoid any abrupt action which might damage your spine.

Resting your left elbow in your right hand, pull it gently toward your right side. Hold and relax.

Repeat using your right elbow.

Place both hands, palms downward, on your chest, with elbows pointing out to the sides.

Circle your elbows forward and backwards three times.

Move your head backward and forward while keeping your chin parallel to the ground.

Tilt your head first to the left and then the right.

Finally, rotate your head, gently and smoothly, first clockwise then counterclockwise. Make sure your neck is so relaxed that your head almost feels about to fall off.

Repeat whenever you experience tension.

Technique #6

Let your head fall forward.

Place the fingertips of both hands at the junction between the upper back and neck. Here you will locate a protruding bone, the seventh cervical vertebra. This is the focus for a complex network of nerves in your back, head, and neck.

Using the middle and index fingers of one hand to apply moderate pressure, circle this bone 20 times. Next locate a slight depression on either side of the spine, leading up toward your skull. The main tendons controlling your head movements are located here.

This area is especially vulnerable to stress and should be soothed using Deep Friction massage (see Chapter 20).

Begin at the seventh cervical vertebra and work slowly up to the base of your skull.

Stretch Away Stress

This procedure can also be used when:

· Driving long distances
· Sitting for lengthy periods behind a desk or computer terminal
· Working in cramped, uncomfortable, conditions

- Standing for long periods, for example serving behind a counter or working on a production line
- Playing a sport, such as squash or tennis, or jogging; they put additional strain on the ankles.

What Goes Wrong

We so often move, sit, or stand very awkwardly, yet are so preoccupied that we fail to notice stress signals from our muscles until we experience serious discomfort.

These exercises can help to counter such stress quickly and easily.

Technique #7

You can perform this exercise most easily while standing or lying down. It can also be done in a chair if there is sufficient legroom to stretch full length.

Focus on your muscles while stretching and imagine all their tension flowing away as you slowly and gently take them to their comfortable limit.

Inhale as you stretch, then exhale while releasing all the tension.

Breathe slowly and deeply, through your nostrils.

Never hold your breath while stretching.

Close your eyes so you can concentrate solely on what your muscles are doing.

Stretch fully and freely, extending your arms above your head while your feet point forward, arching the instep.

Hold the tension for a few seconds, then release.

Repeat three times.

Always loosen tight clothing before stretching and never

stretch within two hours of eating because it diverts blood from your digestive system.

Technique #8

Zenkutsu Dachi derives from the ritualized Japanese Kabuki theater, where it is often used by actors miming fight scenes.

Stand upright. Bend your left knee and extend your right leg behind you. Your arms must remain relaxed at your sides.

Raising and lowering your right heel, make a series of small, bouncing movements. After ten bounces, change and extend your left leg.

Now sit in a chair, stretch out your right leg, and point your toe. Flex your foot by bending it inward. Rotate your ankle for ten seconds.

Repeat six times, then do the same with your left leg.

Technique #9

Holding onto a chair with your left hand, stand with your feet turned out sufficiently to provide excellent balance. Swing your right leg to the right, keeping it slightly bent. Your left, supporting leg should remain straight.

Without pausing, swing your right leg in front of your body, making the movement as fluid as a dancer's, and brushing the ground lightly with your foot while doing so. When touching the ground, your foot should be slightly turned outward.

Swing your leg back to the right again, once more brushing your foot against the ground.

Do this ten times, then repeat with your left leg.

Aromatic Soother

Inhale bergamot or melissa, applied to your handkerchief.

Summary of Technique #3

TAKE A DEEP BREATH.
RAISE SHOULDERS IN SHRUG. HOLD. BREATHE
OUT AS YOU RELEASE.
SPREAD FINGERS. STRETCH AND RELEASE.
MAKE A FIST. RELEASE.
REPEAT THREE TIMES.
TURN HEAD FROM SIDE TO SIDE AND NOD.

Summary of Technique #4

YOUR NECK IS YOUR BODY'S CRUCIAL POINT OF
BALANCE, SO BECOME CONSCIOUS OF ITS POSI-
TION AT ALL TIMES AND TAKE PRACTICAL STEPS
TO REDUCE STRESSFUL ACTIVITIES. WHILE ON
THE TELEPHONE, FOR EXAMPLE, MAKE CERTAIN
TO HOLD YOUR HEAD AND NECK UPRIGHT. SLEEP
LYING ON YOUR BACK WITH YOUR HEAD RESTING
ON A LOW PILLOW OR ROLLED-UP TOWEL.

Summary of Technique #5

REST LEFT ELBOW IN YOUR RIGHT HAND.
PULL GENTLY TOWARD RIGHT SIDE.
HOLD AND RELAX. REPEAT USING YOUR RIGHT
ELBOW.

PLACE HANDS, PALMS DOWNWARD, ON CHEST, ELBOWS TO SIDES.

CIRCLE ELBOWS FORWARD AND BACKWARD THREE TIMES.

MOVE HEAD BACKWARD AND FORWARD, CHIN PARALLEL TO THE GROUND.

TILT HEAD LEFT AND RIGHT.

ROTATE THE HEAD CLOCKWISE, THEN COUNTER-CLOCKWISE, KEEPING NECK VERY RELAXED.

Summary of Technique #6

LET YOUR HEAD FALL FORWARD.

PLACE FINGERTIPS OF BOTH HANDS AT THE JUNCTION OF UPPER BACK AND NECK.

FEEL THE PROTRUDING BONE—THE SEVENTH CERVICAL VERTEBRA. USING MIDDLE AND INDEX FINGERS OF ONE HAND APPLY MODERATE PRESSURE AND CIRCLE BONE 20 TIMES.

LOCATE DEPRESSIONS ON EACH SIDE OF SPINE. SOOTHE USING DEEP FRICTION MASSAGE.

FROM SEVENTH CERVICAL VERTEBRA, WORK SLOWLY UP TO BASE OF SKULL.

Summary of Technique #7

LOOSEN TIGHT CLOTHING.

WHILE STRETCHING, FOCUS ON MUSCLES. IMAGINE TENSION FLOWING AWAY AS YOU STRETCH.

INHALE AS YOU STRETCH. EXHALE WHILE RELEASING TENSION.

BREATHE SLOWLY AND DEEPLY, THROUGH THE NOSTRILS.

NEVER HOLD YOUR BREATH. STRETCH FULLY.

HOLD FOR A FEW SECONDS. RELEASE. REPEAT THREE TIMES.

Summary of Technique #8

STAND UPRIGHT. BEND LEFT KNEE. EXTEND RIGHT LEG BEHIND YOU, ARMS RELAXED AT YOUR SIDES.

MAKE A SERIES OF SMALL, BOUNCING MOVE-MENTS.

AFTER TEN BOUNCES, CHANGE LEGS.

SITTING IN A CHAIR, STRETCH THE RIGHT LEG, POINTING YOUR TOE.

BEND YOUR FOOT INWARD.

ROTATE THE ANKLE FOR TEN SECONDS.

REPEAT SIX TIMES. DO SAME WITH LEFT LEG.

Summary of Technique #9

HOLD CHAIR WITH YOUR LEFT HAND.

SWING RIGHT LEG TO RIGHT, KEEPING IT SLIGHTLY BENT.

YOUR LEFT LEG REMAINS STRAIGHT.

WITHOUT PAUSING, SWING RIGHT LEG ACROSS BODY, LIGHTLY BRUSHING THE GROUND WITH YOUR FOOT SLIGHTLY TURNED OUTWARD.

SWING LEG TO RIGHT AGAIN, BRUSHING AGAINST THE GROUND.

REPEAT TEN TIMES, THEN CHANGE TO LEFT LEG.

24

Controlling Daily-hassles Stress

Just as the mightiest river consists of countless droplets, so most major stress problems are formed from the multitude of apparently minor irritations, frustrations, tensions, and annoyances which can be described as daily hassles.

Although their individual drain on your Stress Resistance reserves may be barely noticeable, they can cumulatively lead to the psychological bankruptcy of Burn Out Stress Syndrome. The procedures described below will help you retain control when you are faced by unavoidable hassles.

Rapid Relaxation

Tension is catching. Somebody with a tight jaw, stiff shoulders, and furrowed brow sends out powerful stress signals to which others respond.

On the other hand, we quickly warm to anyone who is relaxed and at ease. Recent research suggests that people are rated as more empathetic and effective listeners after they have been trained in relaxation.

Technique #10

The secret of success in relaxation is *passive concentration,* focusing your mind on what is happening to you *without* trying to make it happen.

Correct breathing is essential. You should breathe continuously, without pausing between the inhaled and exhaled breath. Each time you breathe out, repeat the word CALM silently to yourself.

Tense—then relax—all the major muscle groups in turn. You can remember the sequence using this mnemonic:

A Soothing *Feeling—My* Body *Has* Peace.

A stands for Arms and hands. Start by tensing the muscles in your forearm by extending your hands at the wrists. Bend them back and feel tension build in the forearm.

Hold for a slow count to five.

Allow your hands to flop down. Feel the tension flowing out of them and notice the difference between tension and relaxation in these muscles.

Now flex your hands at the wrist. Hold for a count of five. Let your hands flop back.

Tense your biceps by attempting to touch the *back* of your wrists to your shoulders. Hold for a slow count to five before allowing them to drop back limply.

Tense your triceps by stretching your arms out as straight as possible. Hold for a count of five. Let your arms flop down by your sides.

S stands for Shoulders and neck.

Shrug your shoulders as hard as you can. At the same time, press your head back against some firm support. Hold for a count of five. Let your shoulders drop and go limp.

F is for Face.

Open your eyes wide. Frown deeply. Screw up your eyes. Hold for five seconds. Relax. Let the lids rest lightly together. Smooth out your brow.

M is for Mouth.

Press the tip of your tongue to the roof of your mouth. Hold for a slow count of 5. Relax and let your tongue rest loosely in your mouth. Clench your jaw firmly. Hold and relax.

B is for Body.

Take and hold a deep breath. Flatten your abdominal muscles as though anticipating a blow. Hold to 5. Let the muscles go limp. Expel air with a gasp before returning to smooth, continuous breathing.

Continue silently repeating the word CALM with each exhaled breath. Notice your relaxation deepening as your body becomes warmer and heavier.

H is for Hips, thighs, calves.

Stretch your legs, toes pointed, and squeeze your buttocks together. Once more hold for a slow count of 5. Relax and let the muscles flop out.

The final letter *P* stands for Picture.

Having relaxed physically, conjure up a soothing mental image which will calm your mind. I will describe how this can be achieved in a moment.

Now tense all your muscles together, using the methods I have just described, and hold that tension for 5 seconds.

Let go.

Flop right out.

Feel all the tension flowing out from your whole body.

This takes around 15 seconds.

For the next 45 seconds—or longer, if possible—conjure up your favorite relaxing image.

At the end of each session, if you have to return to a mentally and/or physically demanding activity, you'll need to wake yourself up again. In Autogenic Training, this technique is called a cancellation.

It's like your first wake-up stretch and yawn of the day.

To do this . . .

Clench your fists tightly.

Briskly bend your elbows and stick your arms out either in front of you or to the sides.

Inhale deeply.

Finally open your eyes and exhale.

It is very important to keep your eyes closed right up to the moment you breathe out if cancellation is to work effectively.

Creating a Stress-free Paradise

Soothing imagery slows your heart rate and raises your body temperature. You can measure its success by taking your pulse before and after you try it. With only a little practice, you should experience a drop of around 10 beats per minute.

Technique #11

While relaxed physically, conjure up a pleasant image. You might imagine yourself lying on a sun-warmed tropical beach or in a lush meadow beside a gently flowing stream.

At first this image is likely to be vague and easily disrupted by intrusive thoughts. With practice, however, most people achieve a vivid and enduring image.

If a worrying idea comes to mind while you are visualizing this scene, imagine writing that thought with a stick on the wet sand at the edge of the tide. Now watch as the ocean laps in and obliterates your problem. As the last trace is washed away, you will experience relief from the worry.

Alternatively, imagine the disturbing idea written on a piece of paper, caught on the breeze and blown higher and higher until it finally vanishes out to sea.

More whimsically, picture a small, friendly creature emerging from the nearby greenery and approaching you timidly. Imagine yourself befriending this animal, which understands everything you say to it.

Confiding all your fears and doubts to this creature while you are mentally and physically relaxed often helps make them seem less daunting and puts difficulties into a clearer perspective. Although it sounds pure Disney, many find this an extremely comforting and helpful visualization.

Make the scene as realistic as possible by employing all your senses. If you are lying on a beach, *hear* the sound of waves gently uncurling on the strand, *smell* the fragrance of wild flowers, *feel* warm sand beneath your body, *taste* the salt on the air.

Create your own personal paradise in which to rest and recuperate on a regular basis.

Warming Away Your Stress

When we are stressed, blood is diverted away from the small vessels directly beneath the skin and sent deeper to the muscles, in preparation for fight or flight. This is why people often go pale with shock.

By reversing the process and sending blood back to these blood vessels, you can reduce your anxiety and stress. This may be achieved by a simple hand-warming exercise. It is a very powerful and valuable procedure which can be used anytime you need to wind down quickly yet unobtrusively—while waiting to present your ideas at a meeting, or during an interview.

There are three ways of warming your hand. Try each and see which one works best for you. At first use your dominant hand (right if right-handed); this makes the exercise easier. If you want to check your skill, use a small thermometer (not a clinical mercury instrument) to measure changes in temperature. You should find a shift of at least three or four degrees after only a little practice. The degree of heating depends on the starting temperature. Obviously, a slightly chilly hand will have more scope for warming than one already close to the core body temperature of 98.6 Fahrenheit.

Technique #12

#1 Imagine your hand growing warmer and warmer. Just by focusing on the idea of heat flowing into your fingers and palm, you may achieve a significant rise in temperature.

#2 Imagine holding your hand before an open fire. Feel the heat from these flames reaching your flesh and raising your temperature.

#3 Place your palm close to—but not touching—your cheek. This is a natural hot spot which radiates a good deal of warmth. Feel this heat gently warming your palm.

Breathing Away Your Stress

Deep, rhythmical stress-reducing breathing depends on having your weight distributed evenly through the spine and legs while you are standing and the spine and pelvis if you are sitting.

Disturbing this balance creates a barrier to efficient breathing. If you are in the habit of leaning across the wheel of a car when driving, or your desk while working, you are placing most of your weight on your elbows and shoulders. This makes them tense and involved unnecessarily in breathing. A hunched posture also pushes your digestive organs upward, limiting the movement of your diaphragm and lower ribs.

Once poor posture has become a habit, lung efficiency is significantly impaired and your ability to cope with high levels of stress is diminished.

Use some kind of external event as a reminder to check your posture and breathing several times an hour. This might be answering the telephone, or finishing one task before starting another. When driving, your reminder could be red traffic lights.

At this time, focus your attention on the way you are sitting or standing and, if necessary, alter your posture deliberately so that your weight is distributed more evenly.

Technique #13

Sit upright comfortably.

Close your eyes.

Place one hand on your chest and the other on your abdomen. Breathe smoothly, slowly, and deeply through your nose.

Pull in your abdominal muscles consciously as you exhale, using your hand, if necessary, to push down your stomach. As you exhale, become aware of your abdominal wall pushing outward.

Practice for a few minutes each day until this becomes your normal pattern of breathing, whether you are sitting, standing, or lying down.

Continue for 30 seconds.

After checking your posture again, resume the task at hand. In just half a minute, your reserves of Stress Resistance Currency will have been increased significantly.

Technique #14

Remove any tight clothing around your neck.

Take off your tie and open the top buttons of your shirt or blouse.

Sit or lie back and relax.

If it is possible, use aromatic massage oil containing either lavender or neroli. Half a teaspoonful is usually enough to cover your face and neck, although you will need more when your skin is especially absorbent. This situation is most likely if you work in an air-conditioned office or have just taken a hot bath.

Using both hands, fingertips closed and touching, start under your chin. Apply firm, gentle strokes, moving outward toward your ears, before returning your hands to the center line. Your wrists should remain supple and your hands pliable. With fingertips only, gently massage your cheekbones, traveling up each side of the nose to your forehead.

Massage your eyebrows before circling your eyes again, then move up your nose and across your forehead to your hairline.

Repeat this soothing action from the bridge of your nose to your forehead several times.

Stroke down your nose, chin, and throat in one continuous line.

Complete the massage by gently stroking your face and neck.

Stomach and Back Stress—What Goes Wrong

Your lower back and stomach mirror tensions elsewhere in your body. Your first experience of anxiety is often a spurt of adrenaline in the pit of your stomach. This early warning of stress can start a rapid spiral of anxiety which affects your whole body.

A strong abdominal wall helps support your lower back and provides better protection for the digestive tract, liver, and kidneys.

The next two exercises not only help you relax and combat stress, but also improve your digestion.

Technique #15

Place your hands on your hips, with fingers touching the groove which runs on either side of the spine.

Apply Deep Friction massage along this groove.

Raise your hands half an inch up your spine and repeat.
Continue as far up your back as is comfortable.

Squeeze the small of your back, on either side, using a kneading movement.

Technique #16

Lie on your back with your knees bent, bringing the heels as close as possible to your buttocks. Placing your hands behind your head, try to sit up and touch your elbows to your knees.

Doing this only once is commendable if you have allowed your stomach muscles to weaken. If possible, repeat six times.

Breathe in as you sit up and exhale as you relax down again.

Do not worry if you are unable to complete this exercise on the first few tries. Persevere and it will become manageable.

Summary of Technique #10

TENSE ALL YOUR MUSCLES.

ARMS AND HANDS—SHOULDERS AND NECK—FACE—MOUTH—BODY—HIPS, THIGHS AND CALVES.

HOLD FOR A COUNT OF FIVE.

LET THE MUSCLES FLOP RIGHT OUT.

FEEL YOURSELF BECOMING MORE AND MORE RELAXED.

CLENCH YOUR FISTS TIGHTLY WHILE BENDING YOUR ELBOWS BRISKLY.

INHALE DEEPLY. OPEN YOUR EYES AND EXHALE.

Summary of Technique #11

TO CREATE YOUR OWN STRESS-FREE PARADISE, VIVIDLY PICTURE SOME CALM, BEAUTIFUL SCENE

SEE, HEAR, TOUCH, AND TASTE THIS IMAGE.

WRITE YOUR WORRIES ON THE SAND. LET THE TIDE WASH THEM AWAY.

Summary of Technique #12

IMAGINE YOUR HAND GROWING WARMER AND WARMER.

IMAGINE HOLDING YOUR HAND BEFORE AN OPEN FIRE.

FEEL THE HEAT RAISING THE TEMPERATURE.

PLACE YOUR PALM CLOSE TO YOUR CHEEK. FEEL THE HEAT GENTLY WARMING YOUR PALM.

Summary of Technique #13

CLOSE YOUR EYES. BREATHE SLOWLY AND DEEPLY THROUGH YOUR NOSE.

PULL IN YOUR ABDOMINAL MUSCLES AS YOU BREATHE OUT.

AS YOU EXHALE, BE AWARE OF YOUR ABDOMINAL WALL PUSHING OUTWARD. REPEAT FOR 30 SECONDS.

Summary of Technique #14

REMOVE TIGHT CLOTHING FROM AROUND YOUR NECK.

USING BOTH HANDS, FINGERTIPS CLOSED AND TOUCHING, START UNDER THE CHIN.

APPLY FIRM, GENTLE STROKES. MOVE OUTWARD TOWARD EARS.

RETURN TO CENTER LINE.

WRISTS REMAIN SUPPLE, HANDS PLIABLE.

FINGERTIP MASSAGE CHEEKBONES TRAVELING EACH SIDE OF NOSE TO FOREHEAD.

MASSAGE EYEBROWS. CIRCLE EYES. MOVE UP NOSE AND ACROSS YOUR FOREHEAD TO YOUR HAIRLINE.

REPEAT SEVERAL TIMES.

STROKE DOWN NOSE, CHIN, AND THROAT IN CONTINUOUS LINE.

STROKE FACE AND NECK GENTLY.

Summary of Technique #15

PLACE HANDS ON HIPS, FINGERS TOUCHING THE GROOVE ON EACH SIDE OF YOUR SPINE.

APPLY DEEP FRICTION MASSAGE.

RAISE HANDS HALF AN INCH AND REPEAT.

CONTINUE AS FAR UP BACK AS IS COMFORTABLE.

SQUEEZE THE SMALL OF BACK, ON EITHER SIDE, USING A KNEADING MOVEMENT.

Summary of Technique #16

LIE ON BACK, KNEES BENT.

BRING HEELS CLOSE TO BUTTOCKS.

HANDS BEHIND HEAD, ATTEMPT TO TOUCH ELBOWS TO KNEES.

REPEAT AS MANY TIMES AS POSSIBLE, UP TO SIX.

25

Controlling Concentration Stress

Working for long periods on intellectually demanding tasks can be far more stressful than you realize. We may become so deeply absorbed in the complexities of the task that messages of distress from mind and body are ignored until it is almost too late. By this time our stress can have risen well above Peak Performance Level, making us far less effective to do that task. To combat our loss of concentration, we may then strive harder than ever to focus all our attention on the problem at hand. The resulting errors and frustrations only compound the problem. Use these exercises to combat stress caused by

· Tasks demanding periods of intense concentration
· Intellectually tough challenges
· Attempting to recall facts and figures against a deadline

What Happens

The inside of the nose is covered with a spongy lining rich in erectile tissue which constantly swells and shrinks. As it swells in one nostril, it shrinks in the other, a cycle which reverses every 95 to 120 minutes. This means there is always either a right or left dominant airflow.

When the air is flowing mainly through the right nostril, we tend to be active, aggressive, alert, and oriented toward the outside world. It is a typically left-brain reaction.

When the air is flowing mainly through the left nostril, we are quieter, more receptive, intuitive, and inwardly directed. That is a right-brain state of mind.

Right-left nostril breathing also affects the way our body works. Research suggests that airflow through the right nostril stimulates the internal organs toward more active states, such as digesting food.

Alternate nostril breathing is designed to restore the balance between right- and left-brain function. This has a calming effect on the mind and helps restore sleep to insomnia sufferers.

Technique #17

Sit comfortably, with your head and neck fairly straight.

Breathe slowly and gently, using your diaphragm.

Press your right thumb gently against your right nostril and breathe out slowly, then inhale.

Lift your thumb to open your right nostril and press your middle finger against your left nostril.

Slowly exhale, then inhale through your left nostril.

Repeat the cycle six times so that you inhale and exhale through each nostril three times.

Repeat for two more rounds, breathing normally between each round.

This makes a total of nine complete breaths through each nostril. Practice each evening before going to sleep.

Technique #18

With both hands, gently stroke your scalp from hairline to back using alternate straight and circular movements. Spreading your fingers across the scalp, apply sufficient pressure to shift the skin slightly across the bone beneath, as if shampooing your hair.

Using small, circular movements, apply fingertip massage to the center of your scalp.

Place three fingers of each hand on either side of your neck and stroke firmly outward, starting just beneath your head.

Continue downward, until the whole neck has been covered. Repeat three times.

All actions must be gentle, flowing, and rhythmic.

Technique #19

This exercise can also be used to reduce stress after

· Prolonged work at a computer terminal
· Reading or preparing lengthy reports
· Lengthy periods of studying
· Driving or flying
· Working under bright lights, especially under artificial illumination
· Fine work which places a strain on the eyes

What to Do

This massage, adapted from one used in the Taoist religion, is especially effective if your work places a great deal of strain on the eyes. It only takes a few seconds to perform and can be used as often as you wish.

Place your index fingers on either side of your nose, directly below the inner ends of each eyebrow.

Apply a firm pressure for ten seconds.

Very gently massage around the eyes using your fingertips in a circular motion.

Repeat three times.

Using your thumbs, apply a gentle pressure to the inner portion of the eyebrow arch, moving outward from the bridge of your nose.

Now apply fingertip pressure to either side of your temple. Starting at the nose, make a series of circular movements around your brow, across the temple, and then back around the cheekbone.

Complete by rubbing your hands briskly together, then placing them over your eyes and forehead.

Feel the warmth from your hands flowing into your eyes and face, easing away any lingering tensions.

Technique #20

After warming your hands by rubbing them together, place them over your face, palms covering the eyes and fingers crossing on the forehead. Avoid pressing against the eyeballs. Relax, shut your eyes, and feel your eyeballs sinking ever more deeply into their sockets.

After a few seconds, start stroking your fingertips outward from the center of the forehead.

Repeat three times.

Place the first two fingers of each hand on your temples and rub gently, using circular movements. After a few moments, move your fingers a little way up or down the temple and repeat this movement.

Aromatherapy

Inhale peppermint either from your handkerchief or from a dispenser.

Summary of Technique #17

CLOSE RIGHT NOSTRIL. EXHALE—INHALE.
OPEN RIGHT AND CLOSE LEFT NOSTRIL.
EXHALE—INHALE.
COMPLETE NINE ALTERNATE BREATHS THROUGH EACH NOSTRIL.

Summary of Technique #18

USING BOTH HANDS, STROKE YOUR HEAD GENTLY FROM FRONT TO REAR.
APPLY SUFFICIENT FINGERTIP MASSAGE, AS IF SHAMPOOING.
MASSAGE YOUR NECK WITH FIRM, OUTWARD STROKES, STARTING JUST BELOW YOUR HEAD.
REPEAT THREE TIMES.
KEEP ALL ACTIONS GENTLE, FLOWING, AND RHYTHMIC.

Summary of Technique #19

USING TIPS OF INDEX FINGERS, APPLY FIRM PRESSURE EITHER SIDE OF THE NOSE, DIRECTLY BELOW INNER END OF EACH EYEBROW.

MASSAGE EYES GENTLY, USING CIRCULAR MOTION.

REPEAT THREE TIMES.

USE THUMBS TO MASSAGE EYEBROW ARCH GENTLY, MOVING OUTWARD FROM BRIDGE OF NOSE.

APPLY PRESSURE EACH SIDE OF THE TEMPLE.

FROM NOSE, MOVE AROUND BROW, USING CIRCULAR MASSAGE MOVEMENTS.

PLACE WARMED HANDS OVER EYES AND FOREHEAD.

Summary of Technique #20

WARM HANDS BY RUBBING THEM TOGETHER.

PLACE OVER FACE, PALMS COVERING EYES, FINGERS CROSSING ON THE FOREHEAD. AVOID PRESSING AGAINST THE EYEBALLS.

SHUT YOUR EYES AND FEEL THE EYEBALLS SINKING DEEPLY INTO THEIR SOCKETS.

STROKE FINGERTIPS OUTWARDS FROM CENTER OF FOREHEAD.

REPEAT THREE TIMES.

RUB TEMPLES GENTLY WITH CIRCULAR MOVEMENTS, USING INDEX FINGERS OF EACH HAND. MOVE AND REPEAT.

26

Dealing with Posture Stress

A great deal of needless and entirely avoidable stress arises from the way we abuse our body daily through poor posture.

The Rapid Stress Control procedures described in this chapter will prove especially helpful if you spend a large part of your working day sitting, walking, or standing for lengthy periods.

What Goes Wrong

Think of your body as a complicated machine, moved by rods (bones) and springs (muscles and tendons). Due to its design, this machine can only operate efficiently—and with a minimum of stress—over a fairly limited range of movements. Outside this range it still functions, after a fashion, but every action becomes less effective and imposes greater stress.

When walking, for example, most people lift their knees too high, pulling—rather than pushing—themselves along. This movement increases stress by inhibiting the body's natural forward motion.

The secret of stress-sparing movement is always to move from the "center" of your body *(hara),* as explained below.

To perform this task, the *hara* is equipped with a broad

sheath of muscle, which enables it to take the strain from other, longer, muscles used to move the limbs.

The *hara* corresponds with the solar plexus, the center of our autonomic nervous system, which regulates stress through the fight-or-flight mechanism. As every boxer knows to his cost, the solar plexus is such an important center of nervous control that a punch here can cause loss of consciousness.

Your solar plexus is situated approximately halfway along an imaginary line passing between the top of your abdomen, directly below the center of the ribcage, and the spine. On a fairly slender person, it is approximately four inches inside the body. The solar plexus is surrounded by many vital structures, including the body's major artery, the aorta. Nerves radiate from here to the arteries, veins, muscles, joints, heart, lungs, stomach, and bowels, enabling the solar plexus to send, receive, and exchange messages between organs and tissues as well as to transmit information to the brain along nerve pathways which include the vagus nerve.

When moving fluidly and harmoniously, tensions are all focused on the abdomen, your body's natural center of gravity, the stable pivot around which other parts can move. This exerts a positive influence on every organ in the body, including the brain itself.

The Japanese, who regard the solar plexus as the center of bodily power, often wear special clothes, such as trousers baggy around the waist, to allow the *hara* to function with greatest efficiency.

Professional dancers also move from their "center," enabling the rest of their bodies to remain relaxed and fluid. In Technique 46 I explain how to control stress by mentally directing heat and light into this region.

Assessing Your Posture

The next time you go walking on a damp, sandy beach, take the opportunity to study your footprints.

An alternative—if messier—method is to coat your feet with water-soluble paint and stand on a sheet of white paper.

Examine the prints carefully.

Are they even, indicating balanced weight distribution, or do they roll to one side?

Do you favor one foot more than the other? Uneven weight distribution can produce aching muscles in both legs and lower back as different groups of muscles are placed under strain trying to compensate for your poor balance.

Notice which foot is normally under the least pressure and make a deliberate effort to push it more firmly against the ground.

As a further check on your posture, stand with your back to a wall, feet at hip-width apart and heels against the wall. Sway back against the wall.

Your shoulders and buttocks should make contact at the same moment.

When one shoulder or buttock makes contact with the wall first, your posture is twisted to the left or right.

If your shoulders touch first, your upper spine is unnaturally arched backward (kyphosis).

If your buttocks make contact before your shoulders, the spine curves too far forward (lordosis). This is likely to result in low back pain.

The hair on the back of your scalp should just brush against the wall. If the back of your head touches the wall, nod forward slightly.

Once you have corrected your posture, move away from the wall and practice maintaining a relaxed stance while walking around using the following exercise.

Technique #21

Stand upright, but relaxed rather than ramrod stiff.

Tuck in your tail and lengthen your entire spine so that it is straight.

This movement pulls in your stomach.

Keep your buttocks taut and flatten your abdomen by pulling in your muscles. This simple procedure alone will greatly reduce the risk of stressful low-back pain.

Raise your ribcage by lengthening your waist, just as you might open an accordion. Let your shoulders drop down and keep them relaxed.

Imagine being a puppet with strings attached to each ear. These strings are drawn upward with even tension, raising your head so that your chin stays parallel with the ground.

Be careful not to tilt your head back; this leads to stiffness in the neck and shoulders.

Keep your neck loose and free.

Think of a pivot running through your ears. Let your head fall forward on this pivot.

Now picture your head being drawn upward again. As you raise your head, simultaneously widen and lengthen your back.

Practice regularly, for 60 seconds at a time, until this is your natural standing posture.

Become aware, while practicing, of tensions anywhere in your body.

Although there will be increased tone in certain muscles, you should never feel uncomfortable or unnaturally strained.

When walking around, keep your weight slightly forward and move with a flowing stride, swinging your legs from the hips. Imagine being pushed forward by a giant hand pressing gently but firmly on your behind.

Because a well-balanced posture reduces anxiety by preventing needless muscle tensions, you should always "ground" yourself before standing to make a speech or presentation. Spend a moment distributing your weight evenly, with your feet a comfortable distance apart. Focus on making firm contact with the floor.

Banishing Sitting Stress— What Goes Wrong

Watch how people sit and you'll quickly realize that the vast majority adopt unnatural, stressful postures which put the spine under considerable strain and are a major cause of low back pain. Among the most frequent faults are

Slouching, so that the spinal column is bent unnaturally.

Crossing the legs, which both twists the spine and impairs the circulation of the blood.

Always make sure that your lower back is fully supported. If necessary, place a small cushion between the lumbar region of your spine and the chair back.

Never remain seated in the same position for too long. Get up and move about regularly.

If you are copy typing, change your copy from one side of the machine to the other from time to time. Make certain that desktops and other work surfaces are at the correct height so that you can work without bending forward.

While driving, sit close enough to the wheel so that your legs are not completely extended on the pedals. Once again, make certain your lower back is fully supported at all times.

Technique #22

At least once an hour, take a 60-second stress break. For 15 seconds, pause and get back in touch with your body. Focus on each of the major muscle groups in turn: ankles, legs, lower back, shoulders, chest, neck, face, arms, wrists, hands, and demand a situation report. There is never any need to ask twice!

As soon as your attention is directed toward a particular muscle, you will become aware whether it is being compelled to function in a stressful and ineffective manner.

Deliberately tense that muscle, using the technique described in Chapter 24.

Hold the tension for 5 seconds, then relax.

Allow the muscle to flop right out and feel it becoming warmer and more relaxed.

Stretch deeply, raising your arms above your head. If possible, do these exercises while standing by a window or in the open air.

Shrug hard three times.

Return to the task at hand.

Banishing Standing Stress

Use this procedure when you are excessively stressed by:

· Having to stand for lengthy periods
· Doing exercise which is more demanding than you are used to

Technique #23

Sit on the floor and bend your right leg, leaving the foot flat.

Starting at the ankle, apply firm, deep, strokes with your hands, moving upward to the knee.

With your thumb and fingers, ease any tension spots with firm rubbing.

Grasp the Achilles tendon between your thumb and fingers. Massage it by moving fingers and thumb in opposite directions.

Repeat for the other leg.

Summary of Technique #21

STAND UPRIGHT. RELAX.

STRAIGHTEN YOUR SPINE. FLATTEN ABDOMEN AND RAISE RIBCAGE.

DROP YOUR SHOULDERS. STAY RELAXED.

KEEP YOUR WEIGHT SLIGHTLY FORWARD WHILE WALKING.

MOVE WITH A FLOWING STRIDE.

SWING YOUR LEGS FROM THE HIPS.

Summary of Technique #22

FOCUS ON YOUR MUSCLES.

DETECT TENSION OR FAULTY POSTURE.

DELIBERATELY TENSE, THEN RELAX AFFECTED MUSCLES.

FEEL YOUR MUSCLES GETTING WARMER AND MORE RELAXED.

SHRUG HARD THREE TIMES.

Summary of Technique #23

SITTING, BEND YOUR RIGHT LEG, KEEPING THE FOOT FLAT.

MASSAGE FROM ANKLE TO KNEE USING FIRM, DEEP STROKES.

EASE TENSION BY FIRM RUBBING.

MASSAGE ACHILLES TENDON BETWEEN YOUR THUMB AND FINGERS.

REPEAT WITH LEFT LEG.

27

Controlling Social Stress

In Chapter 8 I explored some of the ways in which you can
identify and control the stress which arises from working and
interacting with other people. Here I shall describe ways of
keeping your stress levels at optimum when meeting workplace challenges considered stressful by many.

In addition to these specific procedures, bear in mind these
golden rules:

- Recognize the difference between minor setbacks and
  major problems.
- Reflect on how big a problem some current difficulty is
  likely to seem in a year, or ten years, or a century from
  now. Experience suggests that nothing in life matters
  very much, and most things do not matter at all!
- Be yourself and act like yourself. Don't try to be somebody you are not.
- Speak in a calm, relaxed voice and remain physically
  relaxed as well. Even people who are upset or angry
  are likely to mirror this response and calm down. Getting angry yourself only escalates the situation.
- Never phrase your thoughts in a negative manner. One
  mistake doesn't make you a failure.
- Anticipate recurring or commonly stressful encounters,

such as discussing your proposal with a difficult client or employer.

- Find ways to give and receive love. Express your warm feelings regularly for family and intimate friends.
- Feel good about yourself. Remember the last time something really nice happened to you, such as an unexpected pay raise or achieving a major goal. At that time you would not have willingly picked a fight with anybody. Carry that good feeling around even when nothing especially nice has happened.
- Recognize and appreciate the skills, talents, and gifts of others. Thank them for service. Make others feel important, and they will go out of their way to help you. As the great American psychologist William James remarked, "The deepest principle in human nature is the craving to be appreciated."

Confrontation Stress

Confrontation stress arises whenever we have to deal with aggressive or difficult people. The first exercise should be performed prior to any such encounter. It will prove especially helpful if you . . .

- Become breathless during a confrontation
- Suffer from a tendency to hyperventilate under pressure
- Have poor breath control when making a presentation
- Experience giddiness or a sense of unreality in difficult social situations

Technique #24

With practice, this exercise can be done with equal ease standing, sitting, or lying down. At first, practice while lying down on a firm surface. For additional comfort, try placing a pillow under your neck. Stop immediately if you experience any discomfort.

Flop your shoulders like a puppet whose strings have been cut.

Smooth out your brow. Let your tongue rest loosely in your mouth, with teeth slightly apart.

Inhale. Flatten your diaphragm by pushing out with your lower ribs.

Imagine inflating a beach ball inside your abdomen, through a small hole in your navel. Feel the ball growing larger and larger as air is sucked deep into your lungs.

To check that you are doing this exercise correctly, place your hands, fingertips just touching, on your stomach. As your diaphragm flattens, your fingertips should be drawn apart.

Continue for one minute, keeping your breathing slow and deep.

For an alternative exercise, lie facedown, legs a comfortable distance apart, and toes directed outward.

Fold your arms, resting your hands on your biceps. Position your arms to prevent your chest touching the floor. In this posture you have to breathe diaphragmatically.

Inhale slowly through your nose, making sure to expand the abdomen before drawing air into your chest.

While doing so, notice your stomach being pressed ever more firmly against the floor.

Exhale slowly and feel your abdomen being raised from the floor.

Become conscious of this rhythmical movement.

Continue for 60 seconds.

Become aware of the rhythm, of inhalation and exhalation. As I explained above, we normally breathe around 16 times a minute, but this type of deep breathing should be much slower.

Repeat the exercise several times a day, for a week or so, until diaphragmatic breathing has become a habit.

What Goes Wrong

When we are stressed, anxious or upset, our stomach area accumulates tension. Place your hand on a baby's stomach when he is crying and notice how fast he relaxes. Cats and dogs, too, become more relaxed when their stomachs are gently rubbed. Buddhist monks are taught to meditate using an inhaled breath into the stomach, followed by a massage. By the way, this exercise is also excellent for overcoming constipation, a common medical symptom of Type A stress.

Technique #25

Lie down and bend your legs.

Place your right hand on your stomach just below the navel and your left immediately above the navel.

Applying moderate pressure, circle your hands slowly and rhythmically clockwise, following the direction of digestion in the colon.

After 15 seconds, cross your hands so they make contact with opposite sides of the body. Draw your hands together firmly, reducing the pressure gradually so that, when the hands meet in the middle, your fingers are lightly stroking your skin. Repeat six times.

Now focus attention into your solar plexus.

Picture a shaft of golden sunlight flowing into your stomach area and warming it pleasantly.

You are able to regulate this imaginary heat very precisely, to achieve the degree of warmth which feels most comfortable.

Do not become concerned if, at first, plexus warming is hard to achieve.

You may even find your stomach area growing slightly cooler. If this happens, or if you suffer some other mild discomfort, simply stop this part of the exercise and return to your everyday work.

What Goes Wrong

Emotions—especially those that have to be bottled up—exert a significant and negative effect on how we breathe. Typically, the diaphragm and abdominal muscles tense up, pulling the breastbone and ribcage downward. Now, whenever we take a breath, our shoulder and neck muscles must work extra hard to combat this downward force.

The result is fast but shallow breathing and an increased likelihood of *hyperventilation.*

Smokers, especially, are at risk because they get into the habit of sucking air into their lungs using the muscles of the face, throat, and upper limbs, rather than the diaphragm.

The next exercise is especially helpful if you suffer excessive stress . . .

· When coping with strong emotions
· Through bottling up painful feelings
· Due to outbursts of anger or frustration

Technique #26

Slowly breathe in through your nose, comfortably expanding your abdomen first, then your ribcage.

Exhale through your nose more slowly than you inhaled.

Silently repeat the words "relax" and "let go" each time you breathe out.

Imagine those negative emotions flowing from your body with the exhaled breath.

Feel yourself becoming calmer and calmer, more and more relaxed.

What Happens

This is an ancient Chinese breathing technique called *Qigong* (pronounced *chee-goong*). In China there are more than 4,000 different types of *Qigong*. This technique is especially helpful in reducing the stress associated with powerfully arousing emotions such as anger or anxiety.

It is especially effective in reducing stress caused by . . .

· Anger after an aggressive confrontation
· Anticipating a challenging encounter

Technique #27

Stand upright, with your feet sufficiently far apart to ensure a good balance.

Keep looking straight ahead as you exhale.

Breathe in slowly, raising your arms above your head.

Follow the stretch through by rising onto tiptoe at the full extent of your reach.

Feel the stretch going right down to your ankles.

Now imagine a silver thread passing through your spine and lifting you still farther upward.

Continue inhaling while stretching high and higher. At the peak of your lift, start to exhale slowly, allowing your arms to float gently down to your sides as you do so.

Push your palms down and flex your wrists at the end of your exhaled breath.

Repeat five or six times.

What Happens

Many people have gotten into the habit of unintentionally holding their breath when they are suddenly stressed. However unexpected the challenge, it is essential not only to continue breathing, but to ensure that each breath is slow and deep. By doing so, you will quickly gain control over rising stress and return to your PPSL.

Technique #28

Adopt a comfortable sitting or standing posture.

Exhale slowly as you count down from 6 to 0.

Now inhale, equally slowly, and count back up to 6.

Be careful not to hold your breath between breathing out and breathing in.

Picture the sudden stress flowing from your nostrils with each exhalation.

As you inhale, imagine crystal-clear fluid entering your body and helping cleanse it of all traces of that stress.

Each cycle of inhalation and exhalation should take 12 seconds.

Repeat 5 times.

As you reach zero on your final exhalation, feel a sensation of peace, calmness, and control flood through your body. Carry this feeling of tranquility into your next activity.

Summary of Technique #24

LIE DOWN.

FLOP YOUR SHOULDERS. SMOOTH YOUR BROW. LET YOUR TONGUE REST LOOSE IN YOUR MOUTH WITH YOUR TEETH PARTED.

INFLATE AN IMAGINARY BEACH BALL THROUGH A SMALL HOLE IN YOUR NAVEL.

BREATHE SLOWLY AND DEEPLY.

ALTERNATIVELY, LIE FACEDOWN.

FOLDED ARMS PREVENT CHEST TOUCHING FLOOR.

INHALE SLOWLY THROUGH YOUR NOSE.

EXPAND ABDOMEN BEFORE DRAWING AIR INTO CHEST.

EXHALE SLOWLY AND FEEL YOUR ABDOMEN BEING RAISED FROM THE FLOOR.

BECOME CONSCIOUS OF RHYTHMICAL MOVEMENT.

CONTINUE FOR 60 SECONDS.

Summary of Technique #25

LIE DOWN. BEND LEGS.

PLACE RIGHT HAND BELOW THE NAVEL, LEFT HAND IMMEDIATELY ABOVE IT.

CIRCLE HANDS SLOWLY CLOCKWISE APPLYING MODERATE PRESSURE.

AFTER 15 SECONDS, CROSS HANDS TO MAKE CONTACT WITH OPPOSITE SIDES OF THE BODY.

FIRMLY DRAW HANDS TOGETHER.

REDUCE PRESSURE GRADUALLY SO FINGERS ARE LIGHTLY STROKING SKIN WHEN THEY MEET. REPEAT SIX TIMES.

FOCUS ON SOLAR PLEXUS.

PICTURE GOLDEN LIGHT FLOWING INTO THIS
AREA AND WARMING IT.

Summary of Technique #26

BREATHE IN SLOWLY THROUGH YOUR NOSE.
EXHALE THROUGH YOUR NOSE.
REPEAT "RELAX" AND "LET GO" SILENTLY WHILE
BREATHING OUT.
IMAGINE NEGATIVE EMOTIONS FLOWING AWAY
WITH EXHALED AIR.
BECOME INCREASINGLY CALM AND RELAXED.

Summary of Technique #27

STAND UPRIGHT LOOKING STRAIGHT AHEAD.
INHALE AND RAISE YOUR ARMS HIGH OVER
YOUR HEAD.
RISE ONTO TIPTOE AT THE EXTENT OF YOUR
REACH.
IMAGINE A SILVER THREAD PASSING THROUGH
YOUR SPINE AND LIFTING YOU UPWARD.
AT THE PEAK, EXHALE SLOWLY.
ALLOW YOUR ARMS TO FLOAT GENTLY DOWN.
PUSH YOUR PALMS DOWN AND FLEX YOUR
WRISTS AT THE END OF THE EXHALED BREATH.
REPEAT FIVE OR SIX TIMES.

Summary of Technique #28

BE COMFORTABLE SITTING OR STANDING.
EXHALE SLOWLY. COUNT FROM 6 TO 0.

INHALE, SLOWLY, BACK TO 6.

PICTURE STRESS FLOWING AWAY WITH EACH EX-
HALATION.

WHILE INHALING, IMAGINE CRYSTAL-CLEAR
FLUID ENTERING YOUR BODY, CLEANSING THE
STRESS.

EACH CYCLE LASTS 12 SECONDS.

AS YOU REACH ZERO ON YOUR FINAL EXHALA-
TION, CALMNESS AND CONTROL FLOOD INTO AND
THROUGH YOUR BODY.

CARRY THIS FEELING INTO YOUR NEXT ACTIV-
ITY.

28

Controlling Flying Stress

These days more and more business people are having to make frequent and often lengthy flights. Apart from any anxiety you may feel about flying—stress which is best controlled using the relaxation techniques described earlier in this book —jet travel is itself stressful.

You must sit for hours in unnaturally cramped conditions, your lungs abused by inferior air, your stomach by plastic meals from plastic trays, your biorhythms severely disrupted by crossing time zones. The extent of such disturbance is often not fully appreciated, even by seasoned business air travelers.

In a study of 800 frequent travelers crossing multiple time zones, 94 percent were found to have suffered jet lag, and for almost half the consequences proved severe. Ninety percent were sleepy and fatigued on arrival, remaining so up to several days. They remained wide awake at night, but dozed during the day. Poor concentration affected 70 percent, slowed reflexes 66 percent, half reported greater irritability, while 47 percent complained of upset stomachs.

What Goes Wrong

Aircraft air is overheated, dehydrating, and stuffy.

And the longer your flight, the more the air deteriorates. The main loss is among negative ions. Ions are minute particles carrying a positive or negative charge. Positively charged ions stimulate the body's production of the hormone serotonin. This causes aggression, irritability, moodiness, or lethargy. The *mistral,* cold, dry, northwesterly winds, which blow through southern France, are so laden with positive ions that they exert a baleful influence over all exposed to them.

Negative ions, found in the mountains or pine forests, at the ocean, near waterfalls, or beside fast-flowing streams or rivers, produce a tremendous sense of energy and well-being.

Unfortunately, the atmosphere in enclosed, carpeted, air-conditioned places, such as hotels, movie houses, offices, departure lounges, and aircraft, starts out low in negative ions. What few exist vanish quickly when the area is crowded with people.

In an aircraft, recycled air adds to the problem. Oxygen is pumped into the cabin from the front, which means that the flight deck, first-class and business-class areas enjoy the best of the atmosphere while the farther aft one goes through coach, the worse the air becomes. On some flights engineers reduce fuel consumption by shutting down some of the boosters which recirculate the air, causing it to become even stuffier and staler than ever. This is most usual on night journeys, when passengers are likely to blame their fatigue on insufficient sleep and a crowded flight. If flying on work assignments, when your alertness could mean the difference between losing or closing a deal, it always pays to travel business or first class. These classes also allow you to use less-frequented lounges which often provide cleaner, fresher air.

Unless you smoke, avoid the rearmost seats when traveling coach. For nonsmokers this is particularly important on smoking flights, where the aft area is usually set aside for this purpose. Nonsmokers should always travel as far away from the designated smoking area as possible. Sitting even three rows in front of the smokers' section means passively absorbing significant quantities of noxious fumes.

When traveling economy, aim to spend a few minutes every hour as far forward in the aircraft as you can. In a jumbo jet, use toilets immediately aft of business or first class.

What You Can Do—In the Air

Drink plenty of water.

Avoid protein and eat a high-carbohydrate meal, such as pasta, if you want to sleep. This will give you energy for an hour or so, then prepare your body for rest.

If you want to stay awake during the flight, eat protein, such as fish, fowl, or meat, eggs, dairy products, and beans, but avoid carbohydrates. By stimulating the activity-promoting adrenaline pathway, these foodstuffs provide up to five hours of long-lasting energy.

For breakfast after a night flight, take along a high-protein snack, such as cheese, nuts, beans, or chickpeas, or request a high-protein meal from the airline.

For an evening meal, choose the vegetarian menu or avoid the meat.

Eat little on the day before leaving on your trip.

The day before, however, have a big meal. The methylated xanthines in tea and coffee help fight jet lag. Caffeine (tea, coffee, cola, chocolate) theobromine (coffee), and theophylline (tea) belong to this family. Avoid tea and coffee for a day before the flight to clear your system. Then have two or three cups on the morning of your flight if traveling west or in the evening when traveling east.

Stand in the aisle and slowly raise—then lower—yourself on your toes in multiples of 10, changing your weight first to one leg then the other.

What You Can Do—On Arrival

In a city, walk to the nearest park or green space. If it has a fountain or large area of open water, so much the better.

In the countryside, climb the nearest hill, or find running water. By the ocean, take a stroll to the beach.

In your hotel room, open the windows whenever possible. If you can neither open a window nor leave your room, have a warm—not hot—shower rather than a bath. Showers also generate negative ions.

Many professional travelers now carry a portable ionizer with them for use in hotel rooms. This device, smaller than a paperback book, will work in almost any country if suitable adaptors are used.

This simple precaution reduces stress by preventing headaches caused by air conditioning, thus ensuring a better night's rest and boosting energy levels.

Use peppermint or clary sage essential oils to stimulate the system.

The Rapid Stress Control exercises described below will help you do business in the best possible mental and physical shape.

Technique #29

When flying, do this 60-second breathing exercise at least once an hour on daylight flights. During a night flight, do it before attempting to sleep and as soon after waking as possible.

It is best done standing, to make sure that your chest and abdominal muscles can expand freely.

Move as far forward in the aircraft as possible.

Inhale deeply and smoothly through both nostrils.

Feel the air being drawn deep into your lungs.

Hold that breath for a slow count to 5.

Breathe out slowly. While doing so, imagine the cramp and fatigue flowing from your muscles with the exhaled air.

Repeat five times. On arrival at your hotel, do one or more of the following three exercises.

Technique #30

Stand beside a wall and place your outstretched hand on the wall at shoulder height.

Stretch your front shoulder joint by turning your upper body slightly away from the hand. Inhale while holding the position.

Exhale and turn a little farther from your hand. Inhale holding that position.

Exhale and turn your body farther away.

Repeat ten times.

Change sides and complete ten further inhalations and exhalations.

Technique #31

Lying face down, slide your elbows under your body, raising it slightly.

Keep your palms and fingertips in contact with the floor.

Keeping your back, buttocks, and legs relaxed, take all the weight on your elbows.

Inhale and exhale, slowly and calmly, six times.

Technique #32

Lie face down with your arms at your sides.

As you breathe in, start raising your arms toward the ceiling, keeping your elbows bent.

Bring your arms right over your head and back to the floor so long as this can be done without any discomfort.

Time your movements so they are completed at the same moment your inhalation ends.

Reverse the action, concentrating on achieving a slow, smooth, even exhalation as you return your arms to your sides.

Try to make each exhalation longer, and slower, while inhaling at whatever rate you find most comfortable.

Soon you will be able to carry on breathing in this slow, calm manner without having to raise your arms.

Summary of Technique #29

WHILE STANDING AS FAR FORWARD IN THE AIRCRAFT AS POSSIBLE, INHALE DEEPLY AND SMOOTHLY THROUGH BOTH NOSTRILS.

DRAW AIR DEEP INTO YOUR LUNGS.

HOLD FOR SLOW COUNT TO 5.

EXHALE SLOWLY. IMAGINE FATIGUE FLOWING FROM YOUR MUSCLES WITH THE EXHALED AIR.

REPEAT FIVE TIMES.

Summary of Technique #30

PLACE YOUR OUTSTRETCHED HAND ON WALL AT SHOULDER HEIGHT.

STRETCH YOUR SHOULDER JOINT BY TURNING YOUR UPPER BODY AWAY FROM YOUR HAND. HOLD THE POSITION AND INHALE.

EXHALE. TURN FARTHER FROM YOUR HAND.

INHALE HOLDING THAT POSITION.

EXHALE. TURN BODY FARTHER AWAY.

REPEAT TEN TIMES.

CHANGE SIDES AND REPEAT.

Summary of Technique #31

LIE FACEDOWN. SLIDE YOUR ELBOWS BENEATH YOUR BODY, RAISING IT SLIGHTLY.

KEEP YOUR PALMS AND FINGERTIPS IN CONTACT WITH THE FLOOR. YOUR BACK, BUTTOCKS, LEGS ARE ALL RELAXED. KEEP YOUR WEIGHT ON YOUR ELBOWS.

INHALE AND EXHALE, SLOWLY AND CALMLY, SIX TIMES.

Summary of Technique #32

LIE FACEDOWN, ARMS AT SIDES.

BREATHE IN. START RAISING YOUR ARMS TOWARD THE CEILING, ELBOWS BENT.

BRING YOUR ARMS OVER YOUR HEAD AND RETURN TO FLOOR, IF THIS EXERCISE CAUSES NO DISCOMFORT.

COMPLETE MOVEMENTS AS INHALATION ENDS.

REVERSE. BREATHE SLOWLY, SMOOTHLY, EVENLY.

29

Winding Down from Daily Stress

Many of us take our stress home where it can severely disrupt family life, leading to fights, frustration, guilt, and—of course—breeding yet more stress.

Start by calming and centering your mind, using a 60-second meditation. Even this brief period of time is sufficient to place a barrier between work worries and home life. It acts as a psychological buffer, which by helping you unwind creates additional reserves of Stress Resistance Currency, which can be expended dealing with any family problems.

Does Meditation Work?

Because of its supposedly metaphysical associations, many business people who pride themselves on their down-to-earth common sense shy away from meditation. They regard it as something vaguely to do with incense, Sixties flower power, hippies, and Eastern mysticism. In fact, meditation is no more than a technique for concentrating and calming the mind. And research suggests that it can be an effective way to promote mental and physical health. Research published in the *Psycho-*

somatic Medical Journal showed that meditators used health-care facilities 68 percent less than nonmeditators.

Dr. Kenneth Eppley, of Stanford University in California, who studied Transcendental Meditation, found that meditation reduced anxiety twice as effectively as relaxation did.

Research into the effects of meditation on people aged over 80 showed that those practicing meditation had lowered their systolic blood pressure from 140 to 128, were able to think more flexibly, and had better memories.

In another study by Robert Wallace and Herbert Benson of Harvard Medical School, oxygen consumption was found to drop sharply during meditation and rise slowly afterward. Arterial blood pressure remained low throughout the examination with an average BP of 106/57, while levels of lactate in the muscles declined sharply and continued to fall for a few minutes after meditation. This finding is significant because anxiety sufferers experience a significant *rise* in lactate when they are stressed, and patients with hypertension show a consistently higher blood-lactate level.

Heart rate during meditation slows by an average of 3 beats per minute, while brain activity shows a marked intensification of alpha waves, electrical patterns associated with a state of relaxed alertness. This is the very mental condition which meditators claim to develop.

Technique #33

Sit down, half-close your eyes, and focus on a spot on the ground a few feet ahead.

If you meditate in the same place on a regular basis, you may find it helpful to place a colored dot, about the size of a small coin, on some part of the floor or low down on a wall. Suitable colors are yellow, blue, or green, all of which assist in developing a relaxed mental state. If this is not possible, then place a dot on a small card and carry it around with you. Place it on the floor immediately before your 60-second meditation. In addition to providing a consistent point of focus, using your own colored dot will help your mind get into the habit of relaxing and centering. After a time, it acts like the bell used by the Russian physiologist Pavlov, which caused his laboratory dogs to salivate in anticipation of food. Only here your mind anticipates psychological—not physical—refreshment.

Breathe slowly and deeply while concentrating on the spot.

And that's all you need do. For 60 seconds, try not to pay attention to anything but that spot.

Thoughts and images will flash in and out of your mind. Let them. Develop a passive attitude toward these distractions.

As you become aware that your mind has wandered off focus, return it easily and effortlessly to the object of your meditation. Never think about meditating or worry whether you are doing it right or wrong.

You'll find that distracting notions occur less frequently as your meditation skill improves.

Having spent one minute on this exercise, carry your relaxed but alert mental state into everyday life by means of Active Meditation.

Technique #34

Active Meditation means concentrating all your attention on the job at hand. While washing dishes, for example, you might focus on the color of the soap bubbles, or the sensations of warm, soapy, water on your hands.

While walking, focus all your attention on the sights, sounds, and smells of the countryside or park. Smell the wind. What odors does it carry?

Look at the colors of buildings, plants, trees, the sky, clouds. Allow these sensations to deepen and intensify.

Banish Muscle Stress

Having centered your mind, you can now turn your attention to any residual muscle stress resulting from your day's work.

Wrist Stress

Wrist stress is most likely if your job involves repetitive actions, such as typing, operating a computer keyboard, or driving a car or truck. It can also occur following sports, like golf, squash, or tennis, which make extra demands on the wrist.

Technique #35

This exercise comes from China and is called *Huen-Sau,* or Circling Hands. It not only banishes needless tension in your hand and wrist muscles, but also helps make them more supple. You can perform it either sitting or standing.

Stretch out your right hand, thumb tucked in, wrist uppermost.

Bend your wrist, forming a right angle between the hand and forearm. Keeping your elbow as motionless as you can, rotate the hand in a clockwise direction, as far as possible, *without allowing your arm to twist with the hand.* This is most important. Practice will lead to greater suppleness.

When you have turned your hand as far as possible, hold that position for a couple of seconds. Then, very suddenly, make a fist.

While doing so, relax the muscles in your hand and arm. This action takes a little while to master, but brings great benefits.

It helps to practice in a mirror so that the snap of your closing wrist occurs simultaneously with relaxing the muscles.

If done correctly, you will feel tension in your wrist and the underside of your forearm. This indicates that those muscles are being loosened and strengthened.

From the clenched-fist position return to your starting point. Do this twice more.

Now repeat with your left hand, rotating the wrist counterclockwise.

Face Stress

The face is especially vulnerable to emotions because the muscles tense up so easily. While reading or concentrating, you may unknowingly be tensing the corrugator muscle, located above the nose, into a frown. Even this small act of unnecessary tension causes an expenditure of Stress Resistance Currency, depleting your reserves.

Another common focus of tension is the powerful jaw muscle, the masseter. Research suggests this is a problem for around 22 percent of the population. Since the jawbone, like every joint in the body, rests on pads of cartilage, this constant pressure eventually wears the cartilage away.

Long before that, however, you are liable to have worn down your molars through "night grinding," known medically as *bruxism,* which occurs especially during sleep.

Jaw tension can radiate outward to produce headache or earache, as well as the dull facial pain and tenderness which are symptoms of temporomandibular joint (TMJ) disorders.

Technique #36

A quick way of checking how often you tense your forehead is to smooth a piece of Scotch tape across it.

Now, every time you frown, the tape provides immediate

feedback. You may be surprised at how much of a habit frowning has become.

Use this technique to identify occasions when you've gotten into the habit of frowning, such as while reading, talking on the phone, concentrating on a problem, and so on. Now make a conscious effort to smooth out the brow.

You can best release tension in your facial muscles by first deliberately tensing them. Open your eyes wide as though asking a question. Now frown hard, screwing up your eyes. Hold for five seconds. Relax. Let your eyelids rest lightly together. Smooth out your brow.

Headaches can also be eased using massage (see Techniques 18 and 19) and by placing a cool, damp cloth on your forehead.

Technique #37

This exercise, developed at Columbia University, will ensure that the muscles and ligaments of your jaw remain free of tension. It also helps eliminate the pain caused by cramps and spasms.

Slowly open your mouth, as wide as you comfortably can, without forcing your jaw, and breathe in while doing so.

Breathe out while slowly closing your mouth.

Lightly massage the muscles over the joints of the jaw, where it hinges onto the skull.

Repeat 10 times.

Place your fist beneath your chin and open your mouth against mild resistance.

Repeat 12 times.

If the pain, teeth clenching, or night grinding is severe, consult your dentist or doctor.

Shoulder Stress—
What Goes Wrong

Shoulder tension is very common and is frequently associated with tightness in the neck muscles. Many people seem literally to "carry the weight of the world on their shoulders."

We hunch behind the wheel of a car and when seated at a desk or watching television. We shrug our shoulders while talking and even use them to keep our ears warm in winter!

Technique #38

Prevent needless stress by keeping your shoulders loose and relaxed.

When you feel tension, roll your shoulders with an exaggerated rowing-style action.

Shrug hard, drawing your shoulders up toward your ears. Squeeze them together across your chest, then allow them to flop down.

Pull them back, attempting to bring your shoulder blades together.

Repeat three times.

Shrug your shoulders for 20 seconds.

Finally, swing each shoulder backward and forward, while keeping your hands hanging loosely at your sides. Regard your neck as a pivot around which the shoulders are allowed to shimmy, like a belly dancer in full flow!

Try to imitate the action of a dog briskly shaking water from its coat.

Aromatherapy

Moist, rather than dry, heat is best for easing shoulder tension, so take a shower or soak in a warm bath. Use a few drops of ylang-ylang, camomile, or lavender in the water.

Technique #39

Placing your left hand on the right shoulder use a *petrissage* massage technique (see Chapter 20) on the muscles, moving from the side of your neck to the upper arms and applying a firm movement.

Grasping the large muscles of your upper arm (biceps and triceps), move them in a circular fashion.

If the muscles feel especially tense, use your fingertips or the aromatic soother to rub them.

Repeat for your left shoulder using your right hand.

Back Stress—
What Goes Wrong

Pain in the lower back is due mainly to muscle weakness, tightness, or spasm. According to Dr. Zeb Kendrick, director of the Biokinetics Research Laboratory at Temple University, the lower back is the "abused link" in the body. Pain here can arise because of problems with our ankles, knees, hips, and shoulders. High heels are a common cause of low back pain among women, since they throw the body out of alignment.

Technique #40

Lie on your back on the floor, arms at your sides and knees bent, feet flat on the ground.

Draw in your stomach while flattening your spine against the floor so there is no space between your back and the ground. Check this with your hand. Repeat three times, keeping your breath slow and regular.

Now raise your buttocks from the floor by contracting them and using your stomach muscles. Repeat three times.

Bring your knees up to your chest, back flat on the ground. Place your arms around your knees and draw them in as close as possible. Bring your head to meet your knees. Repeat three times.

Staying in the same position, cross your legs at the ankles and grasp each foot, keeping your chin tucked in and your body completely relaxed. Rock back and forth.

Arm and Hand Stress— What Goes Wrong

Repetitive hand work, for instance using a typewriter or computer keyboard, produces considerable tension in these muscles, slowing and undermining performance by making finger movements less accurate. The same problem often afflicts musicians who must have fast and fine control over these muscles. Tennis and squash are among several sports which place significant strain on these muscle groups, as does the operation of certain types of industrial equipment.

Technique #41

With your right hand, rub the length of your left arm, starting at the back of the hand and moving along the outside of the arm to the left shoulder, then back along the inside of the arm to the palm.

Do this briskly and smoothly while applying continuous pressure.

End this stroke as if flicking drops of water from your fingertips.

Repeat 6 times before changing to massage your right arm with the left hand.

Stroke your hand and wrist with palm of the other hand.

Pull every finger from base to tip, finishing each stroke with a brisk snap.

Use the opposite thumb to massage the palm and wrist of your upturned hand, applying a firm, circular movement.

Turn your hand over and repeat, including the knuckles.

Stroke the back of your hand with your palm.

Repeat for the other hand.

Aromatherapy

If you are going out, take a shower rather than a bath to stimulate your system. Inhale some clary sage or peppermint to improve alertness.

Enjoying a Restful Sleep

Foot massage is an extremely effective method for ensuring a good night's sleep. If you have a baby or toddler who refuses to drop off, a little gentle foot massage can work wonders.

Three different techniques for massaging your feet are described below. Use whichever seems easiest and most effective, or switch them around to introduce greater variety into this important massage.

Technique #42

Use a screwing motion to press the fingers of either hand hard into the ball of each foot, in turn.

Repeat with the instep.

Make a ring with your thumb and index finger. Place it over each toe in turn and pull, with a wriggling motion.

Pinch the tip of each toe.

Rub your index finger between each toe.

Smooth the hollows on either side of your Achilles tendon using an upward motion.

Pinch your heel sharply a few times.

Finish by grasping your foot from the side, with both hands, thumbs overlapping the toes.

While pushing your fingers into the sole, simultaneously smooth the top of your foot forward with the fleshy part of each palm.

Repeat with the other foot.

Technique #43

Place your right ankle over your left knee.

Holding your right foot in one hand, rub the entire sole with the fingers of your other hand.

Apply pressure for 5 seconds before moving to a different area of your right foot.

Repeat with other foot.

Technique #44

Using the heel of your right hand, apply Deep Massage strokes while holding your right foot in your left hand.

Massage between your toes.

Pull outward to stretch the muscles and tendons.

Repeat for the other foot.

Summary of Technique #33

SIT. HALF CLOSE YOUR EYES. FOCUS ON A SPOT A FEW FEET AHEAD.

BREATHE SLOWLY AND DEEPLY, CONCENTRATING ON THAT SPOT.

DEVELOP A PASSIVE ATTITUDE TOWARD DISTRACTIONS.

RETURN YOUR MIND TO THE OBJECT OF YOUR MEDITATION.

Summary of Technique #34

CONCENTRATE ALL YOUR ATTENTION ON ANY ACTIVITY.

FOCUS INTENTLY ON THE SIGHTS, SOUNDS, AND SMELLS AROUND YOU.

ALLOW THESE SENSATIONS TO DEEPEN AND INTENSIFY.

Summary of Technique #35

STRETCH OUT YOUR RIGHT HAND, THUMB TUCKED IN, WRIST UPPERMOST.

BEND THE WRIST. FORM A RIGHT ANGLE BE-
TWEEN THE HAND AND FOREARM.

KEEPING YOUR ARM AND ELBOW STILL, ROTATE
YOUR HAND CLOCKWISE.

HOLD POSITION FOR A COUPLE OF SECONDS.
VERY SUDDENLY MAKE A FIST.

RELAX THE MUSCLES IN YOUR HAND AND ARM.
FEEL THE TENSION IN YOUR WRIST AND FORE-
ARM.

RETURN TO STARTING POINT.

REPEAT TWICE MORE.

DO THE SAME WITH LEFT HAND.

Summary of Technique #36

DELIBERATELY TENSE FACE. OPEN EYES WIDE AS
THOUGH ASKING A QUESTION. FROWN HARD.
SCREW YOUR EYES TIGHT SHUT.

HOLD FOR FIVE SECONDS. RELAX.

SMOOTH OUT YOUR BROW.

LET YOUR EYELIDS REST TOGETHER LIGHTLY.

Summary of Technique #37

SLOWLY OPEN YOUR MOUTH WIDE. INHALE
WHILE DOING SO.

EXHALE WHILE SLOWLY CLOSING YOUR MOUTH.

LIGHTLY MASSAGE THE JAW WHERE IT HINGES.

REPEAT 10 TIMES.

PLACE YOUR FIST UNDER YOUR CHIN. OPEN
YOUR MOUTH AGAINST MILD RESISTANCE.

REPEAT 12 TIMES.

Summary of Technique #38

ROLL YOUR SHOULDERS WITH AN EXAGGER-ATED ROWING ACTION.

SHRUG. SQUEEZE THEM TOGETHER ACROSS YOUR CHEST, THEN ALLOW THEM TO FLOP DOWN.

TRY TO TOUCH SHOULDER BLADES.

REPEAT THREE TIMES.

SHRUG YOUR SHOULDERS, RAISING THEM AS HIGH AS POSSIBLE.

CONTINUE THIS FOR 20 SECONDS.

SWING EACH SHOULDER BACKWARD AND FOR-WARD, KEEPING YOUR HANDS LOOSE AT SIDES.

Summary of Technique #39

USE PETRISSAGE ON YOUR RIGHT SHOULDER MUSCLES FROM NECK TO UPPER ARMS.

GRASP THE LARGE MUSCLES OF YOUR UPPER ARM. MOVE THEM IN A CIRCULAR FASHION.

RUB ESPECIALLY TENSE MUSCLES WITH FINGERS OR AROMATIC SOOTHER.

REPEAT FOR LEFT SHOULDER.

Summary of Technique #40

LIE BACK ON FLOOR, ARMS AT SIDES, KNEES BENT, FEET FLAT.

DRAW IN STOMACH. FLATTEN SPINE AGAINST FLOOR.

REPEAT THREE TIMES. KEEP BREATHING SLOW AND REGULAR.

RAISE BUTTOCKS FROM FLOOR BY CON-

TRACTING THEM AND USING YOUR STOMACH MUS-
CLES.

REPEAT THREE TIMES.

BRING KNEES TO CHEST, BACK STILL FLAT ON
GROUND.

PLACE ARMS AROUND KNEES. DRAW THEM
CLOSE.

BRING HEAD TO KNEES.

REPEAT THREE TIMES.

IN SAME POSITION, CROSS LEGS AT THE ANKLES.
GRASP EACH FOOT. KEEP CHIN TUCKED IN AND
BODY RELAXED. ROCK BACKWARD AND FORWARD.

Summary of Technique #41

START AT THE BACK OF THE HAND. RUB LENGTH
OF ARM TO SHOULDER. RETURN ALONG INSIDE OF
ARM.

ACTION SHOULD BE BRISK AND SMOOTH WITH
CONTINUOUS PRESSURE.

END STROKE AS IF FLICKING WATER FROM FIN-
GERTIPS.

REPEAT 6 TIMES. CHANGE ARMS.

STROKE HAND AND WRIST WITH PALM OF THE
OTHER HAND.

PULL FINGERS FROM BASE TO TIP. FINISH EACH
STROKE WITH A BRISK SNAP.

MASSAGE PALM AND WRIST USING OPPOSITE
THUMB. APPLY A FIRM, CIRCULAR MOVEMENT.
TURN HAND OVER AND REPEAT.

STROKE BACK OF HAND WITH PALM.

REPEAT FOR THE OTHER HAND.

Summary of Technique #42

PRESS FINGERS OF EITHER HAND HARD INTO
THE BALL OF EACH FOOT.
REPEAT WITH INSTEP.
TUG AT EACH TOE USING A WRIGGLING MOTION.
PINCH THE TIP OF EACH TOE.
RUB INDEX FINGER BETWEEN EACH TOE.
SMOOTH HOLLOWS ON EITHER SIDE OF ACHIL-
LES TENDON WITH UPWARD MOTION.
PINCH THE HEEL SHARPLY.
GRASP FOOT FROM THE SIDE WITH BOTH HANDS,
THUMBS OVERLAPPING THE TOES.
PUSH FINGERS INTO SOLE AND SIMULTANE-
OUSLY SMOOTH TOP OF FOOT FORWARD WITH
FLESHY PART OF EACH PALM.
REPEAT WITH THE OTHER FOOT.

Summary of Technique #43

PLACE RIGHT ANKLE OVER LEFT KNEE.
HOLDING FOOT IN ONE HAND, MASSAGE RIGHT
SOLE.
APPLY PRESSURE FOR 5 SECONDS BEFORE MOV-
ING TO NEW PART OF THE SAME FOOT.
REPEAT WITH LEFT FOOT.

Summary of Technique #44

APPLY DEEP MASSAGE STROKES, USING HEEL OF
HAND WHILE HOLDING RIGHT FOOT IN YOUR LEFT
HAND.

MASSAGE BETWEEN TOES.
PULL OUTWARD TO STRETCH THE MUSCLES AND
TENDONS.
REPEAT FOR LEFT FOOT.

30

Banishing Stress before It Even Arises

Visualization is an effective technique of dealing in advance with a potentially stressful event. Such a rehearsal will often banish excessive stress before it ever arises, ensuring that you stay at your Peak Performance Stress Level throughout the encounter.

You can gain some insight into the power of visualization with this experiment:

Imagine holding a ripe lemon in your hand.

Now watch yourself cutting off a thick wedge and putting it to your lips. Take a bite.

As the tart taste of the lemon reaches your tongue, feel your cheeks curl and your lips pucker.

Let the image vanish.

Now notice that your mouth is full of saliva.

Merely by imagining yourself cutting and sucking that lemon, you triggered a powerful bodily reaction.

This is not the only physical reaction which mental imagery can produce. Research going back more than fifty years, conducted during the 1930s by physiologist Dr. Edmund Jacobson, demonstrated that if you imagine lifting a heavy weight with your right hand, the muscles in your right arm show increased electrical activity.

Experience suggests that around 10 percent of people have difficulty in forming clear visual images. If you are one of them, do not worry; you do not need an actual mental picture if your thoughts remain clear.

You'll find it easier to visualize if your mind is quiet, your body relaxed, and your eyes are closed. This reduces the risk of interference from unbidden thoughts and provides the creative energy needed for turning an imagined scene into reality.

Before visualizing, set yourself a realistic goal. This is especially important at first since it helps build confidence.

The technique below, called *Zazen,* or "sitting with zen," has been shown to increase the brain's production of alpha waves, which are associated with a state of relaxed alertness.

Technique #45

Sit or lie down comfortably and loosen tight clothing.

Take a deep breath, hold it for a few seconds, then let it go.

Take another, hold it again. This time release the air with a *Haaaaaaaaaaa* sound.

Breathe normally for a few seconds and focus on your breathing.

As you inhale, say to yourself, "I am . . ." As you exhale, complete the sentence by adding "relaxed. . . ."

As you say the word "relaxed," sink more deeply into the chair, rug, or bed. Let gravity take over your body, rather than resisting it as we do most of the time.

Allow each and every fiber of your body to be drawn farther down . . . down . . . down into the support. Feel your mind slowing.

As you inhale, imagine breathing in a warming glow of relaxation. Each time you exhale, picture your tensions, fatigue, and frustrations being breathed away.

Imagine a well, filled with crystal-clear fluid, extending from the top of your skull to the base of your spine. See a gold coin being dropped into this well. Breathe out slowly and visualize the coin drifting slowly downward through the liquid, timing the image so that the coin arrives at the bottom of the well at the same moment you complete the exhalation.

Breathe in slowly and deeply, then repeat with a second coin.

Continue until you have piled ten gold coins, one on top of the other, at the bottom of your imaginary well.

While performing this visualization, focus attention on your exhaled breath and the gently descending coin.

Now imagine yourself performing the stressful activity in a calm, confident, and relaxed frame of mind.

As with the beach scene (Technique 11), it is important to create as vivid an image as possible. See it, hear it, touch, and even taste it where appropriate. If you begin to feel anxiety or uncomfortable stress, return to the coin imagery and relax your mind once again before returning to the activity. In time you'll find that any stress associated with performing it decreases. You may also want to experiment with different types of responses on your own part, to rehearse a number of varying scenarios. Rehearsing in your imagination, while physically and mentally relaxed, makes it easier to cope with stress in real life.

Finish with a further period of soothing mental imagery.

Relaxation and guided visual imagery are not quick fixes. They are skills which can be perfected only by regular practice. But, once mastered, they will prove invaluable allies in managing stress successfully.

Energize Your System

End your day by preparing for tomorrow with a *Chakra* Visualization.

According to the traditions of Eastern medicine, our bodies

have seven *chakras* (energy centers) associated with the endocrine and nervous systems.

Each *chakra* has its own color and is related to specific areas of the body.

The word *chakra* originally meant "wheel," but has since been extended to mean either the period during which the Wheel of Time turns once or centers in the body which collect streams of *pranic* energy.

Chakras are usually depicted as lotus flowers or wheels situated around the spine which represent different levels of consciousness. At the lowest level lies everyday awareness; at the top, cosmic, consciousness.

The first—or root—*chakra,* located at the base of the spine, is associated with the adrenal glands and the color red. It is linked to survival through the fight-or-flight response and so has an especially significant role to play in controlling stress.

The second *chakra,* situated immediately above the genitals, is associated with sensations linked to taste, such as appetite and feelings. It is the sex Chakra and has orange as its associated color.

Chakra number three, found in the solar plexus, is our center of personal power. This *chakra* is used whenever we have a "gut feeling" about somebody or something. Its color is yellow.

The fourth *chakra* lies at the heart and serves to integrate the lower *chakras* into love and harmony. The color of this *chakra* is green.

Chakra number five—the throat *chakra,* associated with the thymus gland—is the *chakra* of self-expression. Its color is blue.

The sixth *chakra,* linked to the endocrine system, is located at the center of the forehead and governs consciousness and awareness. Its color is indigo.

The seventh—brain—*chakra* is situated at the top of the head and is linked to the pineal gland and nervous system. This *chakra* represents the connection between the material and spiritual worlds. Its color is violet.

When we are stressed, our dis-ease shows itself in the part or part of our body controlled by a particular *chakra*. For example a threat to survival, which is often present in a stressful situation, affects the first *chakra,* causing damage to our adrenals and weakening our immune system.

Technique #46

Do this exercise the last thing at night while sitting or lying in a comfortable and relaxed position.

Focus your attention on the first *chakra* at the base of your spine. Imagine the color red, either as a red object such as a dress, a car, sunset, or a diffuse red glow flowing into the lower part of your body.

After a few moments, shift attention to the second *chakra,* in your genital region, and create the color orange in your imagination.

Again use an object or diffuse image of orange and suffuse this area of the body with orange.

Moving upward to the third *chakra,* imagine a yellow image and feel it filling and shimmering around your solar plexus.

Continue through each of the *chakras* in this way, allowing its unique color to flow into that area of your body.

You can remember the color of each *chakra* by thinking of the colors of the rainbow, or using the old schoolroom acronym: Roy G. Biv equals *R*ed *O*range *Y*ellow *G*reen *B*lue *I*ndigo *V*iolet. When you have completed the seventh *chakra,* imagine yourself surrounded by white light.

Feel this light growing stronger and stronger, becoming clearer and clearer. Picture this vivid illumination of pure healing light.

Let the light flood over you, around and through your body, penetrating into every part from the top of your head to your feet. As the light flows through you, imagine it warming and soothing away any remaining stress or tensions.

Summary of Technique #45

SIT OR LIE DOWN COMFORTABLY. LOOSEN TIGHT CLOTHING.

TAKE A DEEP BREATH. HOLD—LET GO.

TAKE ANOTHER. RELEASE WITH A *HAAAAAAAAAA* SOUND.

FOCUS ON BREATHING.

INHALE. SAY "I AM . . ." EXHALE. SAY "RELAXED. . . ."

IMAGINE COINS FALLING DOWN A WELL OF CRYSTAL-CLEAR FLUID, EXTENDING FROM YOUR SKULL TO THE BASE OF YOUR SPINE.

VISUALIZE A GOLD COIN DRIFTING DOWNWARD SLOWLY THROUGH LIQUID, ARRIVING AT THE BOTTOM OF THE WELL WITH THE END OF YOUR EXHALATION.

REPEAT UNTIL TEN GOLD COINS ARE PILED AT THE BOTTOM OF THE WELL.

IMAGINE PERFORMING THE STRESSFUL ACTIVITY IN A CALM, CONFIDENT, AND RELAXED FRAME OF MIND.

FINISH WITH A FURTHER SOOTHING IMAGERY.

Summary of Technique #46

IMAGINE SUFFUSING *CHAKRAS* WITH ASSOCIATED COLOR

RED—BASE OF SPINE

ORANGE—GENITAL AREA

YELLOW—GUT

GREEN—HEART

BLUE—THROAT

INDIGO—FOREHEAD

VIOLET—HEAD

FEEL WHITE LIGHT PENETRATING YOUR ENTIRE BODY, DRIVING AWAY LINGERING STRESS AND TENSION.

ENERGIZE YOUR ENTIRE SYSTEM FOR TOMOR-ROW.

Now go to sleep in a calm and relaxed state of mind and body, renewed by your visualization. Your reserves of Stress Resistance Currency are fully restored. You are ready to face whatever stresses tomorrow may bring: confidently, calmly, and creatively.

31

The Ten Commandments of Stress Control

In my work as a therapist, counselor, and industrial consultant, I have seen far too many once energetic, enthusiastic, and achieving men and women broken on the wheel of runaway stress.

Not only is this uncontrolled stress a tragedy which ruins and wastes the lives of those individuals directly concerned, but it is also a plague which disrupts family life, undermining —often irreparably—relationships between husband and wife, parents and children. It can sap ambition, destroy confidence, ruin careers, and lead to a wide range of drug- and alcohol-abuse problems.

We are right to fear the consequences of uncontrolled stress; they are truly horrendous. But we are no more sensible in this attitude than primitive man was to fear the fire which both warmed his cave and destroyed his crops, cooked his food and devastated the plains on which he hunted.

Stress can be friend or foe.

Turn it into an enemy, and you will be taking on an implacable and ultimately victorious opponent.

Learn to use stress creatively, and it will be your ally.

I hope you have found some of the ideas and strategies by which this may be achieved useful and will practice them.

In conclusion, here are ten of the best pieces of advice I have come across for maintaining your Peak Performance Stress Level throughout life. They will not only aid you in bringing stress back under your control, but help ensure a healthier, happier, and more fulfilling life ahead.

One:

Banish the word "problem" from your vocabulary and replace it by the word "challenge." Block all thoughts starting with the words "should," "ought to," "have to," or "must." Confusing wants with needs generates an enormous amount of unnecessary stress.

Two:

Form judgments on the basis of facts, rather than assumptions. Never assume you know what other people are thinking and feeling. Ask them! Jumping in with both feet by acting impulsively often makes matters far worse. And once a word has been uttered, you can't take it back.

If you are in the habit of sounding off without thinking through the full consequences, visualize a large pot of glue, the kind used around offices and handicraft shops. Picture this glue pot as vividly as possible. Anytime you feel tempted to speak first and think second, imagine using the glue to seal your lips so tight that you can no longer talk.

Instead, just listen. Really listen to what is being said. To be understood, you first have to understand the other person. And this may be done only with your ears—not your mouth. So try putting yourself in the other person's shoes. See the situation through his or her eyes.

The same technique can be used to control anything from angry outbursts to jumping to conclusions. Picture the thought, word, or action being daubed with glue and sealed firmly.

Three:

Reject generalizations, such as "I could never do that," "Life is always unfair to me," "Everybody I know has a better life than I do." Avoid absolutes like "all," "never," "always," "none," "everybody," "nobody."

Four:

Learn *acceptance.* This does not mean always agreeing with everything, or never working to change those things you consider wrong or bad. Accepting a person you find disagreeable does not mean liking or approving of him or her. But acceptance of an emotion—especially a painful one—is the essential first step toward eliminating the discomfort caused by that feeling.

Five:

Take responsibility for your feelings, your actions, and your total life situation. Stop blaming parents, teachers, partner, children, boss, or companions.

Wherever you are, *you* are the one who got yourself there. Wherever you are going, *you* will be navigating that journey. So discard the crutches of blame. Walking is going to be tough at first, but in time your strength will grow to the point where artificial support is never needed again.

Six:

Abandon false hopes which arise from the immature belief that a miracle will somehow save you from laziness, stupidity, or whatever else you regard as the cause of your problems. The sooner you accept that only *you* can shape your life for better or worse, the faster your life is going to improve.

Seven:

Step back and get your problems into perspective. Say to yourself: "However bad I feel now, all this will pass." Use this inner dialogue, no matter how filled with clichés, to distract yourself from negative thinking and distance yourself from the immediate pain. This will put you in a better state of mind to tackle those problems constructively.

Eight:

Simplify your life. Let daisies grow on your lawn. Cut down on home decorating and improvements.

Reduce the intake of useless information.

Read less and read more slowly, savoring the words. Learn to enjoy poetry.

Put more space in your schedule and stop watching your watch.

If you do not believe an activity is worth doing and you get no enjoyment from it, stop doing it.

Nine:

Nature is an excellent therapist. Contemplate greenery. If you live in the city, visit parks and make excursions into the countryside. If possible, walk to work through a park instead of along the street, even when this takes slightly longer.

Grow herbs on your windowsill or in your backyard.

Studies have shown that people relax more quickly and easily in natural surroundings. If this is impossible, find an attractive postcard or poster showing a peaceful natural scene, or take your own photos of a favorite beauty spot.

Spend 60 seconds looking at the picture and imagining yourself actually in those surroundings. Close your eyes after studying the image for 15 seconds and attempt to re-create it in your mind's eye. Pay attention to the other sensations associated with that scene, such as sounds, smells, the warmth of sunlight on your body, the bracing freshness of a sea breeze, the cleansing chill of air from snow-covered mountains.

Try this technique at least three times a day, especially after a stressful encounter or activity. It will help you wind down and will restore your equilibrium.

If it is not possible to have such an image, or carry out such an activity, in your workplace, carry a postcard of the view in your wallet or handbag.

When the sun shines, close your eyes and look toward the light for 20 seconds. Be sure to keep your eyelids shut tight during this exercise. Feel the red glow penetrating your body, warming, relaxing, and healing.

Massage your eyes with your fingertips. You'll find that colors look spectacularly brighter and sharper after you perform this exercise a few times.

If you spend a considerable time doing close work, such as watching a computer screen or reading papers, perform this exercise every hour or so.

Glance up from the document or display screen to any distant object such as the view from your window or even the other end of a large office.

Now look back at the screen or documents.

Repeat six times in order to exercise the muscles which focus the lenses of your eyes. This will keep your eyes strong and prevent eyestrain.

Make a small meditation garden. The most famous Ryoan-ji in Kyoto, Japan, is simply a rectangle of sand with 15 carefully placed stones and some dark moss. Bring home a small piece of nature, such as a piece of wind-smoothed tree trunk, an interestingly shaped stone, a colored shell, and use these as focus points when meditating.

Ten:

Faced with two paths, assume that both are right, instead of seeing them in terms of sure success or certain failure. Every decision we make provides the opportunity to discover more about life. Each new path opens fresh possibilities for mental, physical, and spiritual growth.

Accept full responsibility for your decision. If it doesn't work, change it. Be flexible.

Each time you cope with a situation which previously made you fearful, your self-esteem increases.

Once you realize that you can and will survive, no matter what, your fears will diminish.

As I said at the start of this book, stress can be friend or foe.

Like fire, when used constructively, it is a source of tremendous power and energy. If allowed to burn out of control, however, the results are always highly destructive, frequently fatally so.

I have provided many practical techniques which can quickly and easily be incorporated into the busiest lifestyle. By doing so you can not only improve and safeguard mental, emotional, and physical health but greatly enhance your performance in all areas of life.

None of these techniques can succeed, however, unless you

also develop a positive frame of mind toward the stress of life. Remember there is no place to run and hide from stress. Even if you were to flee to the most remote desert island or climb the highest mountain, stress would seek you out. Its guise would be very different from that encountered in the typical urban or suburban lifestyle but the destructive potential would remain as great as ever.

By following my suggestions for altering the mind set with which you face challenges, you will have taken an important first step toward bringing about those essential changes.

Let me conclude by describing the four most important rules to follow if you truly want to be stressed for success.

One. Be flexible. A driving student once asked his instructor whether it was good to get into the habit of performing a particular action. The expert's response surprised him: "There are no good habits when driving," he answered. By this he meant that no action when behind the wheel should ever be treated in a purely mechanical, habitual way since to do so only invites accidents.

It's the same with life. No event, no situation, no challenge is ever quite the same as the one which went before or the one which will follow. Each is, and should be dealt with, as a unique event.

A newly qualified physician once questioned the diagnosis of an eminent consultant. Furiously he replied: "Young man, I have thirty years' experience with this type of case." To which the doctor is said to have replied: "In my view, Sir, you have had one year's experience which you have repeated twenty-nine times!" Maybe not an advisable response but certainly a perceptive one. So, never fall into a thinking rut.

Two. Be Assertive. Don't allow other people to increase your stress burden by dumping their problems onto your shoulders.

If you are one of those people who hates to say no, however unreasonable the demands, start practicing right away. The first time may be tough. People will be surprised and shocked that you are standing up for yourself. Sometimes they'll get angry, or hurt, or try to use emotional blackmail. Resist the temptation to give in. The second time you say "no" to an unreasonable demand is going to be easier. After a while it will take little or no effort at all.

Three. Be action orientated. Pick up the phone, make the call, write the letter, look up the contact, arrange the meeting, catch the airplane. Determine what needs to be done then DO IT. A wise person once said that if you wait for something to turn up you'll spend your whole life staring at your toes!

Worry is only worthwhile when it offers a springboard for positive action. A practical blueprint for such action can be found within the pages of this book.

Four. Have a Vision. Creative stress is a power source. But power only has value when employed in the attainment of a worthwhile goal. A vision provides that goal.

The best visionaries are those people who are able to draw a conceptual map from where they are now to some imagined future. Who can say: "This is how I will get there . . ."

From now on see yourself as a visionary. As somebody willing and able to make stress their ally on the road to personal and professional success.

Appendix—The Stress Diary

Every day for two weeks record any stressful incidents or situations under the following headings. Copy these onto cards for convenience.

STRESS DIARY—WEEK

DAY: DATE: TIME:
SITUATION:
FEELINGS:
INTENSITY OF FEELINGS:

The Situation
Be as precise as possible since certain environments may make stress more or less likely. Include details of: Who else was present. What they were doing. What you were doing. When it happened. Where it happened.

Time: This is important because you may find yourself becoming more stressed at some particular hour of the day.

Feelings: Include ideas, emotions, bodily sensations, worries and so on, in an arousing situation.

These should be rated on a scale of 1–7, where 1 = Mildly Upset and 7 = Very Distressed.

A typical entry might read as follows:

STRESS DIARY—WEEK ONE

_____ DAY: 1

DATE: 6 May   TIME: 10.25
SITUATION: In the office. Wondering how to fit in all my appointments. Aware of the noise of typewriters and phones. Vice-President asks me to complete an urgent report by lunchtime. I try and explain that my schedule makes this impossible but all my objections are brushed aside.
FEELINGS: Anger and resentment which I have to keep to myself. Fear of losing control over events.
INTENSITY OF FEELINGS: 6

The diary allows you to anticipate high stress situations which can then be rehearsed in your imagination prior to the event so as to reduce their threat. Such rehearsals, carried out in a relaxed state, should be as detailed as possible. Try to hear and feel the scene being imagined, instead of merely visualizing it. Imagine yourself dealing with the challenge in a calm, confident, and successful manner, using information from the diary to create vivid scenarios.